Revenge in Chinatown: The New York City
Mafia/Tong Wars

By Joe Bruno

PUBLISHED BY:
Knickerbocker Literary Services

COVER BY:
Amazon Cover Creator

*****

Chapter One

CHINESE NEW YEAR 1996 – THE YEAR OF THE RAT.

An emaciated young Chinese girl, dressed only in a tattered knee-high smock, sat barefoot on the floor in a tiny threadbare apartment in a dilapidated Mott Street Chinatown tenement on the Lower East Side of New York City. A chamber pot rested on the floor next to her. Her head was shaved, her thin legs exposed, and her almond-shaped eyes screamed fear. Her hands were handcuffed behind her back, and a chain connected to the handcuffs was wrapped around a rusty steam radiator and secured by a Master lock.

She was only in her early teens, but because of her unfeeling fish-like eyes, she looked years older.

From her seat on the floor, she could hear the Chinese New Years' celebration in full force on the Chinatown street below her window. Gongs clanged, and firecrackers exploded, as a crew of costumed Chinese celebrants performed the Chinese Dragon Dance. Hundreds of onlookers cheered, and it sounded like an ancient coliseum when the Christians were fed to the lions.

But as far as the young girl was concerned, the celebrations below could have been a thousand miles away. She had more pressing problems.

Suddenly, she heard voices from the hallway outside the apartment. Two, or maybe three men were speaking loudly in Chinese. They could either be arguing or more likely they were drunk.

She wriggled her hands behind her back, trying to slip her scrawny wrists through the handcuffs. But to no avail.

The voices outside became louder; moving closer to the apartment door. Suddenly, the chatter stopped, and she heard feet shuffle away from the apartment door.

The door opened, and a chubby Chinese gangster wearing jeans, a black leather jacket and a black-satin open-necked shirt slipped inside. His jacket and shirt were open, exposing a Buddha-like belly drenched in sweat. Both his hands were adorned with diamond rings, and a huge piece of jade hung on a gold chain dangling from his neck. He had a saber-like knife stuffed in a sheath attached to his belt. He obviously had been drinking and most-likely snorting coke, which would explain the sweat.

Once inside, he stopped and stared at the girl; lust filling his blood-shot eyes. He smiled, licked his lips, and then he stalked towards the girl. Before he got to her, he removed his leather jacket and flung it onto the floor.

He did not see that she had slipped her wrists through the handcuffs, and her hands behind her were now free.

Standing over her, he said, "The rent is now due. Are you ready to pay?"

He knelt in front of her, removed the knife from the sheath, and laid it on the floor next to him. He unzipped his zipper, slid his pants down, and then he roughly tugged them completely off.

He was now naked from the waist down and ready for some action.

He pulled the young girl down onto her back and savagely jerked off her smock; leaving her totally naked.

With vicious hands, he roughly spread her legs apart. Then, he leaned over her, mounted inside her, and he started pumping away.

They were now face-to-face. Her free hands were behind her, and her legs were scissored around his chubby torso.

The gangster closed his eyes and moaned in ecstasy as he continued to pulsate back and forth inside her.

She laid back and accepted his thrusts; looking intermittently scared and disgusted.

He increased the speed of his movements; moaning louder with every thrust.

As he pumped faster and faster, while moaning louder and louder, she slowly slipped her free right hand from behind her.

Finally, he ejaculated inside her, and then he emitted a primal scream. Exhausted, he collapsed on top of her.

Quickly, she grabbed the knife off the floor and plunged it repeatedly into his back and side, screaming, "You son of a bitch bastard! Now you die! YOU DIE!"

She grunted louder and louder with every plunge of the knife.

As he wriggled in the throes of death, his blood squirted onto her face and into her mouth. She wiped her face and spat the blood into his face.

After he stopped trying to fight back, she shoved him off her, and then she straddled him. They were face-to-face again, this time with her on top.

He started begging, "Please, no more! NO MORE!"

She ignored his pleas and plunged the knife repeatedly into his chest. Her face looked defiant, and she screamed like a banshee.

"FUCK YOU, YOU COCKSUCKER!" she said.

Low growls, like from a beast in the wild, spewed from her mouth.

Then, screaming like a madwoman, she slit his fat throat from ear to ear.

Blood squirted upward, saturating her chest.

In seconds, his dead eyes stood wide open, with his fat belly pointed to the ceiling.

He was one dead motherfucker.

She jumped to her feet and put on what was left of her smock. She picked up his leather jacket, put it on, and zipped up the zipper.

She turned to leave, but then she spun around and spat on his dead face.

"You deserve worse than that, you piece of shit!" she said.

She slowly and quietly opened the door to the apartment and looked both ways. No one was in sight.

She slipped out the door and scampered down the stairs, passing a few startled Chinese tenants. But nobody stopped her.

She sprinted out the front door of the tenement and melted into the festive crowd. She pushed her way to the corner and stared up at the street sign, which said, "Mott and Bayard."

She forced a smile, and then she disappeared into the boisterous crowd.

Chapter Two

Present Day:

Three men in their mid-twenties unloaded a truck inside a dilapidated warehouse on the New York City waterfront. They piled boxes of high-definition DVD players onto the floor. Their names were Paulie Grasso, Jimmy Ryan, and Billy the Mook; three small-time wannabees, each with a brain the size of a pea.

"Marone! We must have close to 500 pieces here," Paulie said.

"Yeah, that's good," Jimmy said. "At $150 each, swag, we're looking at 75,000 clams. That's a nice payday for only a day's work."

Billy bent down and read the fine print on the DVD boxes. He said, "Vafanculo! We're screwed!"

"What do you mean we're screwed?" Paulie said.

"These are Toshiba HD DVD players, not Blue Rays," Billy said.

"What the fuck's the difference?" Paulie said.

"The difference is that these DVD players are obsolete," Billy said.

Jimmy Ryan's mouth fell open, and then he said to Billy, "Are you nuts? What's obsolete?"

Paulie told Billy, "*You're* fucking obsolete. And you're out of your fucking mind. This is a nice payday here."

Billy shook his head and said, "I'm telling you these DVD players are worthless; like Betamaxes were 35 years ago."

"What's a Betamax?" Jimmy said.

"Look, these HD DVD players lost in a shootout with the Blue Rays," Billy said.

"What's this bullshit?" Paulie said. "Is this baseball? Hockey? Shootout! Blue Rays! I still think you're nuts."

"Listen, there's two types of HD DVD players," Billy said. "Toshiba HD DVD players and Sony Blue Ray HD DVD players. The Sony's were better and cheaper, so Toshiba stopped making HD DVD players."

"So what!" Paulie said. "That makes the Toshibas we have more valuable because there's less of them. That's the law of supply and demand."

"Except for one little problem," Billy said. "Neither player is compatible with the other. And now all the HD DVDs are only made in the Blue Ray format."

"So, you're telling me we have 500 Toshiba HD DVD players and no tapes to play on them?" Paulie said.

"Yeah. That's basically what I'm tellin' you," Billy said.

"So, we're screwed," Jimmy said.

"Basically," Billy said.

Paulie grabbed Billy by both shoulders and said, "Basically, I'd like to split your fucking skull."

Billy pushed off Paulie's hands and said, "Hey, don't kill the messenger. I'm just telling you the truth here. Plus, there's this new thing called 'streaming' where you can watch movies without a cable box if you have a smart TV."

"You ain't smart enough to have a smart TV," Paulie said.

"I was smart enough to see we have 500 useless DVD players

here," Billy said.

Paulie brushed his fingers through his black curly hair and said, "My luck's been so bad lately if it were raining tits, I'd get hit in the head with a flying cock."

"Cock what? What cock?" Jimmy said. "We ain't fags here."

"Just start putting this shit back into the truck," Paulie said. "My head's killing me. I need four Advil and a stiff drink."

"Now that you mention it, I've got a load of hydrocodone I'm selling," Billy said. "How about a few dozen or so? I'll give you a good deal on them."

"Just start loading the fucking truck," Paulie said.

Paulie picked up a box and placed it into the back of the truck. Then he said, "You know Eddie Coyle was right when he said, 'Life is tough, but it's tougher when you're stupid.'"

"Who's Eddie Coyle?" Jimmy said. "Irish, right? He's from the 4ᵗʰ Ward, right?"

"He's your mother's petunias," Paulie said. "Just start loading the fucking truck."

Chapter Three

Paulie Grasso sat, along with his father, Pete, and his sister, Lisa, at the dining room table in their house in Bay Ridge, Brooklyn. Paulie and Pete chowed down on huge plates of spaghetti and Italian meat sauce like this was their last meal before a date with the electric chair. Lisa, looking like she'd rather be anyplace else in the world, pecked at her food like a bird.

Pete's wife, Rita, tottered into the room carrying three large plates of meatballs, sausages, and braciole. She balanced the three plates between her arms like she's been doing this all her life; which she has. She put the plates in the middle of the table next to the huge family plate of spaghetti and plopped down into her chair.

"Ah, I finally get to sit," Rita said. Then, she turned to her daughter and said, "What's the matter with you? You're eating your food like it's cough medicine."

"Nothing, Ma. I'm just not hungry," Lisa said. "I had nightmares last night, and I just couldn't sleep."

"Nightmares? What did you dream about?" Paulie said.

Without looking up from her food, Lisa said, in a flat monotone, "I dreamt that you were my brother."

Before Paulie could reply, Johnny Grasso, Paulie's older brother, sauntered into the room. He wore a dark-blue pinstriped Brione suit, Ralph Lauren silk shirt, and a Hermes silk tie. He took off his suit jacket, exposing a .38 caliber police special sitting in a shoulder holster.

Johnny sat at the kitchen table and said to Lisa, "I have nightmares that Paulie was my brother, too. But in *my* dreams, I just fucking shoot him."

Rita pointed her fork at Johnny and said, "Hey! No cursing at the dining room table."

"Sorry, Ma," Johnny said.

"And take off that gun," Rita said. "You know the rules. No guns at the kitchen table."

"You made that rule for your son, Paulie the criminal; not for your son, Johnny the cop," Johnny said. "I'm a decorated New York City Police Detective."

Rita pointed at Johnny's gun and said, "Lose the gun! Right now!"

"Okay, okay. Keep your shirt on, Mom," Johnny said.

Johnny stood from the table. He removed the shoulder holster with the gun still in it and placed in on a nearby credenza, which was decorated with pictures of saints and a statue of the Virgin Mary. A crucifix hung on the wall behind the credenza. Above the crucifix, sat a photo of John F. Kennedy. Next to Kennedy's photo was one of Frank Sinatra.

Johnny sauntered back to the table. He sat down, picked up a fork, and started shoveling food into his mouth.

Paulie turned to Johnny and said, "Hey, big brother, I have a nice present for you."

Johnny stopped his fork filled with spaghetti inches from his mouth and said, "Yeah? What is it?"

"I have DVD players for the entire family," Paulie said. "They're the new ones that play high-definition DVD's."

"Are they Toshibas?" Johnny said.

"Yeah. Toshibas," Paulie said. "Brand new and still in the box."

"They're paperweights," Johnny said.

"Paperweights? No. They're high-definition DVD players," Paulie said.

"Doorstops."

"Doorstops!" Paulie said. He put his hand up like a cop stopping traffic. "Stop! Enough of this bullshit!"

"Hey, no cursing at the kitchen table," Rita said.

"Listen. Sony controls the high-def DVD player market," Johnny said. "They call them Blue Rays."

Rita said, "Aren't the Blue Rays a baseball team?"

"No, Ma. That's the Blue Jays," Johnny said. "Now, getting

back to Paulie's useless DVD players." He turned to Paulie and said, "Throw them away. All the high-def DVD's come in a Blue Ray format now. Those Toshibas are obsolete. Like Betamaxes."

"Your father bought me a Betamax about 30 years ago," Rita said. "I still use it to prop open the door in the attic."

Pete looked up from his food and said, "How about we change the subject? I get sick when I think of the Betamax that I bought."

"Good idea," Johnny said. "I just want to enjoy my food."

Lisa said to Johnny, "Did you hear, they found another dead prostitute; this time in an alleyway on Crosby Street? I think that's number four. Are you involved in that investigation?"

"No. Homicide has that one," Johnny said. "I'm working on the Chinese gang problem. Besides, that's the first prostitute murder in the Fifth Precinct. The three other murders happened in different precincts uptown."

"Yeah, that's scary," Lisa said. "A girl just can't walk the streets these days."

"Hey, sis," Paulie said. "We're talking about hookers here. A hard-working girl like you has nothing to worry about."

"Maybe. But it still gives me the creeps," Lisa said.

Pete turned to Johnny and said, "So, how's things in my old Little Italy neighborhood? Or should I say Chinatown?"

"Same old, same old," Johnny said. "The Italians are a dying breed in Little Italy. The Chinese have basically taken over the entire neighborhood. The dead bodies that do turn up; they're all Chinese."

Paulie made the sign of the cross and said, "There *is* a God."

"See? That's why we moved out to Brooklyn in the first place," Pete said. "The Chinks basically pushed us out of our own neighborhood. Uncle Vito says he's up to his neck in Chinks."

"Uncle Vito is also up to his neck in cash," Johnny said. "The fact is, he has an ongoing agreement with the Chinese Tong boss, Duk Tang."

"You sure it's not Peking Duck?" Paulie said.

Johnny shot Paulie a dirty look, and then he said, "Uncle Vito controls the Italian rackets, and Duk Tang controls the Chinese rackets. Every New Years', they exchange fat envelopes as a show of good faith."

"Uncle Vito should put a bomb in the next envelope he gives

to that Chink," Paulie said.

"But there's one thing Uncle Vito doesn't get a cut from," Johnny said.

"What's that?" Pete said.

"The smuggling of illegal Chinese aliens from China into America," Johnny said. "It's big business now, run by Chinese gangsters called Snakeheads."

Rita made the sign of the cross and said, "What a horrible name: Snakeheads."

"There's Cantonese Snakeheads, and then there's Fukienese Snakeheads," Johnny said. "They don't even speak the same language, but they all work together. All they care about is making money."

"How does this operation work?" Pete said.

"The contacts are made in China," Johnny said. "Poor Chinese Immigrants pay as much as 50 large a head to get smuggled into the United States. From China, they go from place to place by boat and usually wind up somewhere in Canada. From there, they get smuggled into the United States; either in big vans or sometimes in the trunks of cars."

"Marone! 50 large!" Paulie said. "Those Chinks must be making a lotta cabbage."

"More than you think," Johnny said. "The Snakeheads sometimes even use old fishing trawlers to smuggle the Chinese immigrants in; fifty, a hundred, two hundred people at a time. They stop a few miles off the coast of New York City, and then they are transferred to the mainland by small boats."

"There must be ways for us Italians to scarf down some of that cavolo," Paulie said.

"Forget about it," Johnny said. "It's a complete Chinese operation. No Lo Fon involved."

"Screw those fucking Chinks!" Paulie said. "They're stuffing Little Italy with millions of those slanted-eyed bastards. They're making it miserable for us Italians to live in our own neighborhood. Some way they gotta fuckin' pay."

"Hey, no cursing at the kitchen table," Rita said.

"So, how do you know so much about these Snakeheads?" Pete said.

"My partner Norman is Chinese," Johnny said. "His parents

were born in China. He knows all about the Snakeheads and how they operate."

"I think Norman is a snake, too," Lisa said. "But he's not bad-looking for an Asian."

Pete stared at his daughter, hard, and said, "Hey, I don't want no half-breeds in this family."

"There must be a way for us to make some money off those Chinks," Paulie said.

"Yeah. Sell them those fagese DVD players you wanted to stick us with," Johnny said.

"Fuck you!" Paulie said.

Pete, Rita, and Lisa screamed in unison, "Hey, no cursing at the kitchen table!"

Chapter Four

As Chinese dragon music blared in the background, two Chinese gang members rained punches and kicks on a fallen male Chinese teenager under the Manhattan side of the Manhattan Bridge, near the East River.

Ah Kay, the leader of the gang, grabbed the Chinese teenager by the hair, and he pulled him to his knees.

"Where's the rest of my money?" Ah Kay said.

Whimpering, the Chinese teenager said, "I pay! I pay! I pay 20 thousand dollars already! I get the rest soon!"

Xin Lin, Ah Kay's right-hand man, backhanded the Chinese teenager across the face.   Then, he said, "One week. 30 thousand dollars. Or we come back."

"I try! I try!" the Chinese teenager said.

Xin Lin landed a roundhouse right to the Chinese teenager's face. The Chinese teenager fell flat on his back; blood oozing from his nose and mouth.

"Call China! Call your relatives!" Ah Kay said. "Tell them to pay our man in Guangzhou."

The Chinese teenager sat up, and he wiped the blood off his face with the back of his hand.

"Okay. Okay. They pay," he said. "Right away, they pay."

Ah Kay landed a savage kick to the Chinese teenager's face.

The Chinese teenager spat teeth, and more blood flowed out both sides of his mouth. Then, he fell unconscious onto his back.

Ah Kay smiled, and then he said to Xin Lin, "That was fun. Let's do this again in seven days."

An unmarked police car negotiated the traffic on West Canal Street on the outskirts of Chinatown. Johnny Grasso was driving, and his partner Norman Wong sat next to him. Sinatra crooned on the car radio, and Norman sang along with Sinatra. Norman's English was impeccable; there was no trace of a Chinese accent.

"Ah, what I'd give to be Italian," Norman said. "The food. The songs. The women. Your sister, Lisa."

"Forget about my sister, Lisa," Johnny said.

"What do you mean?" Norman said. "The girl's obviously crazy about me."

"Yeah, she's crazy alright," Johnny said. "But my father's crazier. And he's got a gun."

"I don't plan on dating your father," Norman said.

Johnny gave Norman the evil eye, and then he wisely changed the subject.

"Looks like another dead hooker showed up last night," Johnny said. "This one they found in the Fifth Precinct on Crosby Street."

"So what?" Norman said. "That's one less whore the city's

got to worry about."

"You always were a sensitive guy," Johnny said.

Norman pulled out a wallet from his rear pants pocket. He removed a photo of a beautiful Chinese woman, and he handed the photo to Johnny, saying, "Now, this is a real woman; not like the pigs turning up dead."

Johnny looked at the photo, and then he said, "Nice looking chick. Is this your sister?"

"No, my sister's so ugly, she'd break the camera," Norman said. "This is my friend Ping. She's a businesswoman in Chinatown."

"So, why do you keep a businesswoman's picture in your wallet?" Johnny said.

"To impress jerkoffs like you."

"Scumbag."

Norman put the photo back into his wallet and his wallet back into his rear pants pocket.

"How about we cut a deal?" Norman said. "A double date. Me and your sister, Lisa. And you and Ping."

"A double date?"

"Sure. What have you got to lose?"

"What have I got to lose?" Johnny said. "My balls! That's what I've got to lose. If my father found out I set up my sister with a Chink, he'd cut off my balls."

"This is a gorgeous Chinese girl I'm dangling in front of your face," Norman said.

Johnny thought for a moment, and then he said, "Ok. You've got a deal. But I'll deliver my sister on this date. If my old man finds out about you and her, he'll have a shit fit."

Norman sang with Sinatra on the radio; *"I'VE GOT THE WORLD ON A STRING, SITTING ON A RAINBOW! GOT THAT STRING AROUND MY FINGER!"*

Johnny sang, *"WHAT A WORLD! ... WHAT A LIFE!"*

Norman sang, *"I'M IN LOVE!"*

Norman weaved the unmarked police car, like a maniac, west on Canal Street. The police light on the dashboard was flashing and the siren blaring; for no particular reason except that Norman figured he was a cop, and he could do anything he pleased.

Chapter Five

The Atlantic Ocean, just ten miles from New York Harbor, was pitch black, and the rain poured down in sheets. In the background, just visible, were the bright lights of New York City.

A small fishing trawler rocked back and forth in the furious rainstorm, and a small rowboat bobbed violently next to the trawler. A disheveled Chinese man sat in the rowboat. He held an oar in the water on each side of the rowboat, which looked like it might capsize any second.

Ah Kay stood on the deck of the trawler, and Xin Lin stood next to him. Suddenly, two Chinese gangsters dragged three Chinese male prisoners onto the deck of the trawler and threw them down onto the floor. As Xin Lin grabbed one prisoner and pulled him to his feet, Ah Kay motioned for the man in the rowboat to move the rowboat closer to the trawler.

"Jump! Now!" Xin Lin said to the frightened prisoner.

The man hesitated, and then he jumped safely into the rowboat.

Ah Kay grabbed the second prisoner and said, "You too! Jump!"

The second prisoner also jumped safely into the rowboat.

Xin Lin grabbed the third prisoner, and he said, "Now you! Jump!"

The third prisoner jumped, but he mistimed his leap, and he fell into the raging waters.

The three men in the rowboat tried to save the drowning man. They grabbed his arms, but they were too weak to drag him into the rowboat.

As the drowning man struggled to swim, a man in the rowboat offered him an oar. The drowning man grabbed the oar, but as the other men struggled to pull him into the boat, a wave crashed into the drowning man. He fell back into the water; losing his hold on the oar in the process.

The rowboat tipped, and it almost capsized. The three men in the rowboat screamed.

A gunshot blasted from the trawler. The drowning man took a bullet in the chest, and he sank below the surface.

Holding a smoking gun, Ah Kay looked down at the rowboat, and he said to the three men, "Row to shore! Now!"

The three men, each wielding an oar, rowed away into the darkness.

Ah Kay turned to Xin Li and said, "That bullet was part of the cost of doing business."

"Yeah, but what a waste of a bullet," Xin Lin said. "And

what about the money we just lost for the creep we just killed? We were supposed to smuggle him into the United States?"

Ah Kay smiled and said, "We've already got twenty grand from his family in China. We'll collect the rest from them."

"How? The guy's dead."

"We'll collect the money before they find out he's dead."

"Suppose they find out he's dead before we get our money?"

"Then, we'll just kill one family member at a time until we get all our money," Ah Kay said. "Believe me, after we kill one; the others will pay."

Then, he spat into the ocean and said, "That's the best part about being a gangster. Killing people."

The two Chinese gangsters exchanged high fives, and then they pulled their heads back and laughed like hyenas.

Inside Forlini's Italian Restaurant on Baxter Street just below Canal Street, Johnny and Norman sat on the right side of the room in a corner booth, and Lisa and a Chinese businesswoman, Ping, sat facing them.

Red leather booths lined the perimeter of Forlini's, and several tables sat in the center of the room. Numerous gold-framed portraits decorated the walls.

Three prominent portraits depicted: *"An old man smiling," "A young woman singing,"* and *"An old man playing the violin."*

All of Forlini's seats were filled with happy customers, and a line of more than a dozen people waited for a table by the entrance.

Forlini's male patrons wore sports jackets and suits. They were obviously professional men; not gangsters. The women were decked out in expensive suits, dresses, and skirts. Their diamond rings and necklaces sparkled. They were high-class women; not a "mob wife" in the joint.

Ping's jet black hair flowed down her back to her waist. Even though they were indoors, she wore her trademark black-framed Christian Dior sunglasses.

Dinner was done, and the waiter put the check on the table.

Derek Forlini arrived at their table. He was the part-owner, along with his cousin, Joe.

"Can I buy you people an after-dinner drink?" Derek said.

"Absolutely," Johnny said. "Make it four doubles of your finest."

Norman picked up the check and scanned it. Then, he said to Derek, "I know all about inflation, but your prices look like telephone numbers. What did we do? Break a window or something?"

"Come on, the check is cheap considering all you ate," Derek said.

Norman handed Derek a credit card and said, "Ok. I'll let you extort me; just this one time."

"I'll be back with the on-the-arm after-dinner drinks," Derek said. "All Sambucas?"

Lisa and Ping said yes, and Johnny said, "Make mine a Black Buca."

"Black Buca for me, too," Norman said.

Derek said, "Two regular Sambucas for the lovely ladies. And two Black Bucas for the bad guys."

Johnny said to Derek, "Tell your story walking. We want to be alone with the ladies, and I know what a snake you are."

After Derek left the table, Lisa said, "Boy, you guys are a tough audience."

Johnny smiled, and then he said to Ping, "So, Norman tells me you own a travel agency in Chinatown."

"I do," Ping said.

"That's how I met Ping; arranging a trip to China to see my family," Norman said.

Johnny said to Ping, "Well, maybe I can use you in the future."

Ping smiled and said, "I hope you're talking about my travel agency."

"What else would I be talking about?"

Ping quickly changed the subject, when she said to Johnny, "Tell me about your job. Any interesting cases lately?"

"To be quite honest," Johnny said. "the Fifth Precinct doesn't have much crime, except for organized crime; both Italian and Chinese."

"Well, that should keep you busy."

"Not really. The problem is that the Chinese people traditionally won't report crimes to the New York City Police Department. They won't even talk to Chinese-American police officers like Norman."

"That's right," Norman said. "A few years back, a Chinese store owner on Canal Street filed a police report complaining about being shaken down by the Vietnamese Born to Kill Gang. Before we could do anything about it, he was shot and killed right in front of his family; in his own store, no less."

"I remember that," Ping said.

"Since then, the Chinese store owners won't complain to us about anything," Johnny said. "The Chinese gangs have scared them away."

Derek arrived at the table holding a tray containing the four drinks.

"Look who's here," Norman said. "Artie Buco."

"Who's Artie Buco?" Lisa said. "Maybe you mean Osso Buco."

"You know, Artie Buco from the Sopranos," Norman said.

"I don't like the opera," Lisa said.

Derek distributed the drinks to the proper people. And then he said, "Two double Bucas. Two double black Bucas. Anything else?"

"Yes, the lovely sight of you leaving our table," Johnny said.

Derek smiled, and then he said, "Enjoy."

Derek went back into the kitchen.

Lisa said to Johnny, "Tell Ping about the Snakeheads."

"No, she doesn't want to hear about that garbage," Johnny said.

"But I do," Ping said. "Please tell me."

"Norman's more the expert about them than I am," Johnny said.

"These Snakeheads smuggle illegal Chinese immigrants into this country," Norman said. "Then, they torture them if they don't pay the $50,000 fee on time."

"Yes, but why do they call them Snakeheads?" Ping said.

"Because, as legend has it, when the illegal immigrants sneak through the fences, they look like little snakes from a distance," Norman said.

"That's stupid," Lisa said.

"And so is this conversation," Johnny said. "What do you say we split?

"No. Tell me more about the Snakeheads," Ping said. "I'm interested."

"What's to tell?" Johnny said. "The Fujianese gangs used to control all the Snakehead trade. Now we have the Cantonese Big Circle Boys to contend with."

"Big Circle Boys?" Lisa said.

"Yeah, that's what they call themselves," Norman said. "But if you ask me, they're the Big 'Circle Jerk' Boys."

Ping shook her head and said, "Both Norman and I are Cantonese. He should know the Big Circle Boys are no joke. They're dangerous people."

Johnny stood from the table and said, "You guys ready? My father has a stopwatch on my sister, Lisa."

"Don't listen to him. My father's asleep already," Lisa said.

"Yeah, he's asleep," Johnny said. "With a gun on his lap."

Norman stood and said to Johnny, "You're right. I don't want no trouble."

Lisa and Ping also stood, and Lisa said, "Ok. Let's blow this popsicle stand."

The two couples cheerfully glided out of Forlini's and into the outdoor parking lot next door. Norman handed his parking ticket to the attendant.

While he was waiting for the attendant to bring him his car, Norman said, "I'll drive Lisa home to Brooklyn."

"Ok. But remember my father. Be smart," Johnny said. "Don't drop my sister off in front of our house. Drop her off around the corner where he can't see your car."

The attendant brought Norman his car, and Norman said, "How much do I owe you?"

"Nothing," the attendant said. "Derek took care of it for you already."

"And you're always breaking his balls," Lisa said.

Norman tipped the attendant a fiver. Then, he told Lisa, "The Forlinis are good people; I've always said that. I just like to have fun with Derek."

Norman opened the front passenger's door for Lisa, and Lisa

kissed Johnny's cheek.

"Remember, go straight home," Johnny said. "Don't let Norman get cute with you."

"Norman get cute?" Lisa said. "I'll break his nose."

Lisa slid inside the front passenger seat of the car, and Norman said to Johnny, "Tough chick. I like them tough."

"Remember, take my sister straight home," Johnny said. "No gallivanting. My father's a nut."

Norman strutted around the front of the car. He opened the driver's door and slipped behind the wheel.

Lisa said to Norman, "Don't listen to my brother. My father's a pussy cat."

"Yeah, a Bengal tiger pussycat," Johnny said.

Norman put the car in gear and exited the parking lot.

As Norman's car pulled out of the parking lot, Johnny said to Ping, "I'll walk you home. 50 Bayard Street, right?"

"How did you know where I live?" Ping said.

Johnny put his arm around her shoulder and said, "I'm a cop, remember? I know everything."

Johnny and Ping headed south on Baxter and made a left on Bayard. Five minutes later, they stopped in front of 50 Bayard Street, near the corner of the Bowery. The Manhattan Bridge sparkled in the background.

50 Bayard Street is a luxurious high-rise apartment building, set in the midst of 100-year-old tenements.

"Would you like to come up for a nightcap?" Ping said.

"That nightcap sounds great, but I have an early day tomorrow," Johnny said. "Can I get a rain check?"

"Why, of course."

"No expiration date?"

"Within reason."

"I'll take the rain check," Johnny said. "You fill in the expiration date."

Johnny extended his right hand; expecting a handshake.

Ping took his hand, and then she kissed Johnny on both cheeks.

"Call me," Ping said.

"I don't know," Johnny said. "When someone kisses an Italian man on both cheeks, something bad usually happens."

"Not if a Chinese girl does the kissing," Ping said.

"I'll take your word for it," Johnny said.

Ping gave Johnny a big smile, and then she said, "Toodles." She turned around and strolled into 50 Bayard Street.

As she sashayed away, Johnny stared at her shapely rear end and said under his breath, "Madone."

Slightly in love, Johnny sauntered towards the Manhattan Bridge.

Norman's car was parked on a desolate Brooklyn Street, a few blocks from Lisa's family's house. The windows were steamed; like something hot and heavy was going on inside the car.

In the back seat, Norman and Lisa were kissing passionately. Suddenly, he grabbed her breast and roughly tried to unbutton her blouse.

She slapped his hand. Then, she shoved him away with two hands to his chest.

"I said stop!" she said.

Norman took his hands off Lisa and said, "I guess I got a little carried away."

Lisa, her face encased in anger, said, "If you keep that up, you will get carried away."

"Okay. My bad," Norman said. "It won't happen again."

"You're damn right it won't happen again!" Lisa said.

Lisa pushed open the back seat door.

"Where are you going?" Norman said.

"I'm walking the rest of the way home," Lisa said. "It's only a few blocks. By the way, Johnny is right about my father. He's not exactly in love with the Chinese."

Lisa exited the car and slammed the door behind her. She quickly strutted down the block; her high heels clicking on the pavement.

Norman got behind the wheel and followed her. He pulled the car alongside her, rolled down his window and said, "Come on. Get in. I'll drive you home."

"Not a chance in hell!" Lisa said.

Lisa picked up her pace; her heels clicking louder and faster.

"Okay," Norman said. "Good fucking night!"

Lisa's face screamed anger. She shot Norman the Italian Salute, and then she broke into a trot and disappeared around the corner.

Norman's face contorted with rage. He gripped the steering wheel like he wanted to turn it into sawdust.

"Fuckin' Guinea bitch!" Norman said.

Chapter Six

It was high noon, and several goombahs hung out in front of an Italian Member's Only Social Club on Mulberry Street. Paranoid about law enforcement and its powers, they repeatedly whispered into each other's ears; like English spies in Nazi Germany.

Inside the club, wooden tables and chairs dotted the floors, and an espresso machine sat on top of a small bar.

Numerous photos decorated all four walls. Some were photos of famous Italian boxers. Others were photos of famous Italian singers. One was a stock photo of Pope Pius XII, and another was a photo of Sophia Loren wearing a loincloth.

As is usual in most New York City Italian Member's Only Social Clubs, Frank Sinatra crooned on the jukebox.

Paulie Grasso sat at a corner table, across from Carlo

Landano, a made-man in the Mafia. Both men picked from a plate of Italian cheeses and Italian cold cuts.

"Those fuckin' Patriots destroyed you," Carlo said. "Your weekly tab is up to 50 thousand clams. What are we gonna do here?"

"Brady gets hurt and is out for the fuckin' year," Paulie said. "I got no fuckin' luck."

"Where do you come off betting dimes anyway?" Carlo said. "That's way over your head. I would never have approved the bets if it weren't for your Uncle Vito."

"Don't worry. I'm good for it," Paulie said.

Carlo shoved a large chunk of provolone into his mouth, and he said while still chewing, "Look, I'll do you a favor. I'll front you the fifty grand. At two points a week, instead of the usual three; as a favor to your Uncle Vito.

"Thanks. I consider it an honor."

"But no more dime bets on a game. Two hundred clams. Tops."

"Done."

Carlo stuck his forefinger under Paulie's nose and said, "And don't go bettin' with any other books. That will definitely get my attention, and I will not be happy."

"Jeez. How can a man get even betting only 200 bucks a game?" Paulie said.

"Be a man. Go out and steal for a living. Make a score, like every other man in this 'thing of ours.'"

"I'm not even officially in this 'thing of ours,'" Paulie said. "I'm still making my bones."

"Keep up your stupid gambling and your bones will be in a fuckin' coffin," Carlo said.

"Speaking of scores," Paulie said. "I've got this great idea. It involves shaking down the Chinks. It could be a big moneymaker for us."

"Big moneymaker?" Carlo said.

He shoved a chunk of Italian salami into this yap and said, "Talk to me. I'm all ears."

Two Chinese gang members stood like sentinels by the outside front door of a Chinese coffee shop on Pell Street in the heart of Chinatown. They had nasty sneers on their faces; like they'd like to bite the heads off rattlesnakes.

Inside the coffee shop, Carlo sat a table with the portly Tong leader Duk Tang. There was a brandy snifter on the table in front of each. Paulie and Ah Kay sat at a table next to them; playing bodyguard for their bosses. Each stared darts at the other hoping the other blinked first.

Carlo took a sip of this drink, and then he said, "I tell you, Duk, this is a damn good brandy."

"Actually, my friend, it's Cognac; Louie XIII," Duk said. "It was a gift from your Don Vito last New Year's."

"Right ... Cognac," Carlo said. He took a sip, smacked his lips, and said, "You know, we've had a wonderful relationship, the Chinese and the Italians in Chinatown, for over 100 years now.

"Yes, my dear friend," Duk said. "All the Mayors of Chinatown have maintained strong relationships with our Italian colleagues. Mock Duck in the early 1900s. Uncle Seven. The honorable Benny Ong. Man Bun Lee. And myself. Ours were, and still are, very strong and profitable relationships, indeed."

"And every New Years' we exchange envelopes as a show of good faith and prosperity," Carlo said.

"Yes, good faith and prosperity."

"We each handle our own people's needs, but we share in the profits. To a certain extent, I mean."

"My friend, I sense some reticence in your voice," Duk said.

"Well, there is this little problem with your smuggling of illegal Chinese immigrants into Chinatown," Carlo said. "You haven't let us wet our beaks, not even a little bit, in this huge moneymaking operation of yours."

"What does that have to do with the Italians?" Duk said. "Now, if the situation were reversed, and it were you smuggling in your own people, we would not expect a share of your profits."

"Well, that's one way to look at it," Carlo said. "But the way we see it is this. You've been smuggling in thousands, maybe even tens of thousands of illegal Chinese every year; crowding our streets so bad you can't walk two feet without bumping into a Chinaman. These are the same streets we both share to do our business."

"So, the streets are a little more crowded," Duk said. "How is that an issue?"

"It's not just that," Carlo said. "It's these stupid shootings; Chinese gangsters charging into restaurants and shooting up the joints like maniacs. White people are now afraid to come into Chinatown. Bottom line. That's bad for all our businesses."

"Oh, I hardly think that's the case," Duk said.

"Look at it this way," Carlo said. "We have only a handful of Italians still living in Little Italy. But you have millions of Chinese in our streets and more coming in every day. They feed your bellies but not ours. When's the last time you saw Chinese people eating in an Italian restaurant? Like how about never."

"You are right about that," Duk said. "But you must understand your Italian food is far too rich for our taste and so fattening, too."

"Looking at you, Chinese food must be pretty fattening, too," Carlo said.

"Yes, I intend to lose a few pounds," Duk said. "Too many Lo Mein dishes. Too many eggrolls."

"Us Italians figure that because your millions of Chinese here in our neighborhood don't feed us a penny, we need the white tourists to make our businesses prosper," Carlo said. "But your crazy Chinese gangs are chasing those white tourists away. No white person in their right mind wants to get a belly full of lead just for walking the streets of Chinatown."

"And this is coming from our friend, Don Vito?" Duk said.

"Of course, it is," Carlo said. "I wouldn't discuss something like this with you without the okay from my boss."

"My first indication is to say no," Duk said. "But let me think this through, and I will get back to you."

"How long will this take?" Carlo said.

"Maybe a few days; a few weeks. Who knows?" Duk said. "I was not expecting this."

Duk and Carlo stood at the same time. They shook hands, but they were not smiling.

Carlo turned to Paulie and said, "Come on. Let's go."

Paulie stood. He shot Ah Kay a stare like he'd like to strangle the Chinese bastard. Paulie sauntered towards the front door. He stopped, turned around, and said to Ah Kay, "Be seeing you around, pal."

Ah Kay smirked and said, "Any time. No problem."

Carlo and Paulie exited the coffee shop; neither were in the best of moods.

Duk said to Ah Kay, "That was not a conversation I expected. And I did not appreciate Carlo's attitude."

"Me neither," Ah Kay said. "What do you propose we do?"

"Nothing. Absolutely nothing," Duk said. "We'll just wait. And when the time is right, we will make the first move. The Chinese now outnumber the Italians ten to one in this neighborhood. They would be foolish to engage us in a war they cannot possibly win."

Duk and Ah Kay took a seat at Duk's table. Duk poured them each a shot of cognac. They both downed the cognac in one huge gulp.

Ah Kay slapped his hand down on the table and said, "Fuck those greaseball bastards!"

Carlo and Paulie exited the Chinese coffee shop, and they pushed their way past the two Chinese guards. They hurried down the street and stopped at a black Lincoln Town Car.

Carlo looked back over his shoulder at the Chinese coffee shop and said, "That did not go the way I expected."

"So, what's our next move?" Paulie said.

"It might be time for us to land a sucker punch," Carlo said. "A huge sucker punch from way out in left field."

Paulie opened the front passenger's door for Carlo, and Carlo slid into the front passenger's seat. Paulie walked around the front of the car, and he opened the driver's door and got behind the wheel.

While the Lincoln exploded out of the parking spot, burning rubber, the two Chinese bodyguards in front of the Chinese coffee shop smirked, then they hit each other with a loud, smacking high-five.

It was just before dawn, and three Chinese gang members sat in a Hummer headed west on Canal Street towards the Holland Tunnel.

There was light car traffic, and no pedestrians were in sight. Rap music blared from their car radio, and there was a slice of light visible on the horizon.

A black sedan, looking like an unmarked police car, screeched out from a side street, and it T-Boned hard into the Hummer.

Three men, with stockings over their faces, sprinted from the unmarked sedan. Two of the men fired handguns, and the third brandished a fiery machine gun.

Heavy gunfire blasted into the Hummer.

The Hummer's windows shattered, and bullets riddled the Hummer's doors, roof, and hood.

The Chinese gang members inside the Hummer flinched violently; like puppets with their strings being yanked one way, then another.

One at a time, the three Chinese gang members stopped flinching; until all three keeled over dead.

The three gunmen sprinted toward a waiting car, and they piled inside.

The car sped away.

Inside the car, the three shooters removed the stockings from their heads and the gloves from their hands. They were Paulie, Billy the Polark, and Jimmy Ryan. Carlo was the getaway driver.

"Good work, boys," Carlo said. "Now, let's get something to eat."

"How about the Market Diner?" Paulie said.

"The Market Diner closed for good last year," Carlo said. "I know a diner on Ninth Avenue that's open 24 hours."

"How about that diner in Jersey right on the other side of the Holland Tunnel?" Paulie said.

"What, are you nuts?" Carlo said. "There's cameras in the Holland Tunnel."

"I want a big fat cheeseburger," Jimmy Ryan said.

"No burgers," Bill the Polark said. "I've put ketchup on my burgers, and I've seen enough red for tonight."

"Fuck 'em!" Carlo said. "We're going to Wo Hop on Mott Street; right in the heart of Chinatown. It's been open 24 hours a day for the past hundred fuckin' years."

"Yeah. Fuck 'em!" Paulie said. "It's still our fucking

neighborhood."

"You're fuckin' right it is," Carlo said. "We're going to Wo Hop, and we ain't paying a fuckin' cent either. I'll just put it on my tab."

"You have a tab at Wo Hop?" Paulie said.

Carlo smiled and said, "I do now."

Chapter Seven

The sun had just risen on Canal Street. Traffic was starting to build, and pedestrians began hustling to work.

The bullet-riddled Hummer and the unmarked car were roped off in the street in a crime scene. Three sets of paramedics carried three sheet-covered bodies. They put the bodies into three separate ambulances.

Johnny and Norman flashed their badges to a cop guarding the crime scene. Then, they stepped under the yellow crime-scene tape and approached a young uniformed policeman.

Johnny said to the young policeman, "Were you the first on the scene?"

"Yes, sir," he said.

"I'm Detective Grasso," Johnny said. Then, he nodded towards Norman and said, "This is my partner Detective Wong. What do you have for us?"

"Three dead Chinese gang members," the young policeman said. "Shot dead in the Hummer."

"How do you know they were gang members?" Norman said.

"They all had guns in their possession. But they were killed before they could draw their weapons."

"And the other car?" Johnny said.

"Could be an accident," the young policeman said. "But I don't think so."

"Anything else?" Norman said.

"Yes. The dead men had a combined ten thousand dollars in cash on them; give or take a few twenties. And a large stash of drugs, too."

"Make sure all the cash and drugs are vouchered properly. Capice?" Norman said.

"Absolutely."

Norman said, sarcastically, "Yeah, right."

"Were there any witnesses?" Johnny said to the young policeman.

"There was an old Chinese woman coming out of the subway," the young policeman said. "She said she saw three masked men jump into a waiting car. She said she thought they were white. But this woman is as old as dirt and not a very reliable witness."

"Thanks. Keep us posted," Johnny said.

"Will do, Detective Grasso."

"Remember, voucher all the money and the drugs," Norman said to the young policemen. "I'll be checking up on you."

As Norman and Johnny exited the crime scene, the young policeman seethed.

Johnny and Norman walked back to their unmarked car, and Johnny said, "That wasn't nice what you said to that cop. He's one of us."

"Fuck him," Norman said. "Hey, maybe it was just a case of drug-induced road rage. Case closed."

"What about the witness?"

"Old Chinese woman. Probably half-blind. Can't say her statement is too reliable."

"I hope you're right," Johnny said. "What we don't need now is a race war in Chinatown."

"That would not be good."

"You look a little under the weather," Johnny said.

"Couldn't sleep last night. Upset stomach," Norman said. "Must have been something I ate at Forlini's."

"Forlini's food was fine. You must have a stomach virus or something."

"Yeah, maybe."

"You hungry now?"

"Yeah. Let's go get some Chinese breakfast," Norman said. "Some dim sum, maybe. There's a great joint on Pell Street."

"Okay. But no Chinese chicken feet," Johnny said. "Just the sight of them makes me sick."

"How about some cha siu bao?"

"Steamed or baked?"

"The steamed taste mushy," Norman said. "Let's go for the baked."

"Ten-four," Johnny said.

The two detectives got into their unmarked car; Norman at the wheel. He made a screeching a U-turn and headed east on Canal towards Chinatown.

Paulie strutted through the front door of Carlo's Members Only Social Club on Mulberry Street. As Dean Martin crooned on the jukebox, several meaty thugs stood at the bar sipping espresso. Several other hoods sat at two tables, playing cards. Two of them were wearing 1940s-type fedoras on their fat heads.

One of the hoods, an especially corpulent one, was Philly Guns; the mob boss, Vito Morrone's, bodyguard.

"How's it going, Philly?" Paulie said.

Philly Guns put down his cards, and he nodded towards the back and said, "I'm doing good. Carlo's waiting for you in the back room."

Paulie knocked on the back room door, and Carlo said, "The door's open."

Paulie entered the back room, and he spotted Carlo sitting at the small round table. Carlo was sipping espresso and scanning the sports pages in the *New York Post*.

"Close the door behind you," Carlo said. "And lock it."

Paulie closed and locked the door. Then, he said to Carlo, "What's up?"

Carlo pointed to the chair opposite him and said, "Have a seat."

A boombox sat on Carlo's table. Carlo turned it on and pumped up the volume. AC/DC blared from the boombox, and the music was so loud, Paulie put his hands over his ears.

"Whoa!" Paulie said. "Why so fucking loud?"

"Because the walls have ears," Carlo said.

Paulie sat in the chair opposite Carlo, and he handed Carlo an envelope.

Both men leaned across the table; their noses almost touching.

"First week's vig," Paulie said.

"Don't forget to keep it coming every week," Carlo said.

"No problem," Paulie said. "I have a few things in the works."

"Let me remind you, any money you kick up to me from a score is not a vig payment, Carlo said. "Both are separate obligations."

"Of course, I'm not stupid," Paulie said.

"Anyone who says they are not stupid, they're usually stupid," Carlo said.

"Whatever," Paulie said.

Carlo made a shooting motion with his thumb and forefinger.

"Did you lose those things?" Carlo said.

"Dead and buried," Paulie said. "I dropped them off the Staten Island Ferry into the drink."

"I heard there was a witness," Carlo said. "Some old Chinese lady coming out of the subway."

"So what?" Paulie said. "Slanted eyes have trouble seeing; especially old slanted eyes."

"Yeah, you're probably right," Carlo said. "But who the fuck knows what people are thinking?"

"Thinking and knowing are two different things," Paulie said.

"Not in this 'Thing of Ours,'" Carlo said. "Mob guys are naturally paranoid. If they even think you did something wrong, they'll whack you out in a second."

Suddenly, there was a big explosion in the front room, and

Paulie and Carlo dived under the table. In seconds, the back room was filled with smoke and screams emanated from the front room.

Paulie slowly opened the door leading to the front room, and through the dense smoke, he saw small fires flickering throughout the room. He also saw that the tables and chairs were mere splinters and that several mobsters lay moaning on the floor. Many of them were bleeding from head wounds.

Philly Guns tried to stand, but he fell flat onto his face.

Carlo rushed into the room, and he grabbed Paulie by the arm.

"Quick! Out the back door!" Carlo said.

"But we gotta help Philly Guns," Paulie said. "He's my uncle's right-hand man."

"Fuck Philly Guns!" |Carlo said. "He's so fat we can't pick him up anyway. Besides, there might be another bomb coming, and we could get killed ourselves. Plus, I owe the fat fuck twenty grand."

"But Philly Guns is still alive," Paulie said. "And he's a made guy."

"I'm a made guy, too" Carlo said. "And I ain't getting killed by acting stupid."

Carlo pulled Paulie into the back room, and he opened the back door leading into the backyard.

"Let's get the fuck out of here right now while we can," Carlo said.

Then, he grabbed Paulie's arm and pushed him out the back door. Carlo followed.

They dashed down a narrow alley, and then they jumped over a fence into the backyard of the adjourning tenement. They sprinted through the back door of the adjourning tenement and through the hallway. Neither being in the best of shape, they stumbled through the decrepit building and staggered out the front door.

Outside, they glared down the street towards the Italian social club. They saw through the smoke that the front of the building was ablaze, and in the background, they heard fire engines blaring.

Carlo and Paulie dashed down the block to the parked Lincoln Town Car. They jumped inside, and Carlo got behind the wheel.

Carlo quickly backed up the Lincoln and screeched back to the corner.

At the corner, Carlo shifted the car into drive. The Lincoln burned rubber around the corner and barreled down the next block.

"Fuck, we just saved our own lives," Carlo said. "We weren't responsible for what happened in the front room."

"I hope my uncle sees it that way," Paulie said. "Otherwise, we're both up shit's creek."

Chapter Eight

Johnny strolled through the front door of the Triple Eight Travel Agency on the Bowery, just below Canal Street. Ping sat at her desk in the back, shuffling paperwork.

Johnny sauntered over to her desk and said, "Had lunch yet?"

Ping looked up at Johnny. She smiled and said, "Not yet."

"I'm buying," Johnny said.

"Sounds like a plan," Ping said.

"Chinese food okay with you," Johnny said. "We are in Chinatown, you know."

Ping stood and put on a full-length black-leather coat.

"No. I only eat Italian food," she said. "Meatball egg foo young."

She kissed his cheek and said, "But I have to make a stop first."

Johnny extended his arm and Ping took it. They strutted out of the office like they didn't have a care in the world.

They strolled south on the Bowery arm-in-arm, and they

stopped in front of a storefront that served as a Chinese food kitchen for poor Chinese people who couldn't afford to eat properly.

They slipped inside, and they saw a line of Chinese woman waiting to be served at a long cafeteria-style counter. As Chinese chatter reverberated throughout the room, the food was distributed by two elderly Chinese men.

Ping led Johnny past the food counter to a door marked "private." She knocked on the door, and a male voice said, "Come in."

An elderly Chinese man greeted them at the door.

"This is Housie," Ping said to Johnny. "He helps fund this food kitchen."

Housie said to Ping, "How come you're not spooning out food behind the counter?"

"I have a date for lunch," Ping said. "Housie, meet Detective Johnny Grasso. From the 5th Precinct."

Johnny shook Housie's hand and said, "My pleasure, sir."

Housie bowed and said, "Venerable New York city policeman, I am very honored."

Ping handed Housie an envelope. Housie took the envelope and peeked inside.

"Sister Ping, you are so kind," Housie said. "I see your travel agency business is doing very well."

"Just like in the Sanitation Department," Ping said. "Business is picking up."

"Now, we can purchase some fresh meat to go along with the vegetables and rice we are presently serving," Housie said.

"I have to leave now," Ping said. "Lunch with Detective Grasso. Then, back to the old grind."

"You could eat here," Housie said.

"I could," Ping said. "But I'm not going to let Detective Grasso off the hook so easily."

Housie turned to Johnny and said, "If you go to a Chinese restaurant, stay away from the pork fried rice."

"The pork in the fried rice isn't really cat," Johnny said. "Is it?"

"Millions of stray cats in New York City," Housie said. "Cheaper than pork."

"Don't listen to Housie," Ping said. "I'm Chinese from

Chinatown. The restaurants I frequent, take my word for it, they don't serve cat."

"But some restaurants do?" Johnny said.

"Some yes, some no," Housie said. "You have to be Chinese to know which ones serve which. Don't forget, eating cat is allowed in China. The locals like it even better than eating pork or chicken."

"That's all a figment of Housie's imagination," Ping said.

As Johnny and Ping turned to leave, Housie yelled out, "Meow!"

Ping laughed and said to Johnny, "Quick, let's get out of here before he corrupts you."

Ping grabbed Johnny's arm and pulled him out of Housie's office.

Johnny and Ping approached a small Chinese restaurant on the Bowery that looked more like a coffee shop. In the fogged restaurant window, fried ducks and chickens hung by their necks.

"This is it," Ping said.

"I hope we have better luck than those chickens and ducks in the window," Johnny said.

They entered, and Johnny saw that the joint was nothing but a narrow, dingy dive. The wall menu was written in Chinese, and so were the table menus. All the patrons inside were Chinese, except for Johnny.

A waiter directed them to a small table in the back by the kitchen's swinging doors.   After they took their seats, Johnny glanced back at the kitchen's swinging doors and said, "These are real Bob Uecker seats. The best in the house."

"Who's Bob Uecker?" Ping said.

"Never mind," Johnny said. "He's just an old baseball player who always sat in the worst seats in the ballpark."

Johnny glanced at the wall menu and then at the table menu, and then he said, "I guess you're ordering. I don't read Chinese."

"Don't worry," Ping said. "I eat here frequently. I've probably have had everything on the menu already."

The waiter brought over two cups of hot tea and two glasses of water.

Ping spoke to the waiter in Chinese, but to Johnny, it might as well have been Greek.

After the waiter left the table, Johnny said, "What did you order?"

"I'm not telling you," Ping said. "It's a surprise."

"That's what I'm worried about," Johnny said. "Believe me, I get enough surprises just doing my job."

"Don't worry," Ping said. "The food is great here."

Johnny said, "Tell me something. At the soup kitchen we just left, all the people eating there were women. Why is that?"

"Those women work 12 to 16 hours a day at one of the many sweatshops in Chinatown, for much less than minimum wage," Ping said. "They cannot afford to eat properly on what they earn. So, we take care of them."

"So, where are all the men?" Johnny said.

"The men work in restaurants all day, doing menial tasks for pennies an hour," Ping said. "But they eat for free, mostly cheap meatless rice dishes. We get a few men early in the morning at the soup kitchen before they go to work. It's their best meal of the day."

"We're talking about illegals here. Right?" Johnny said.

Ping smirked, and then she said, "You're a regular Carnac the Magnificent."

"Come on," Johnny said. "Are things so bad in China that these poor people would leave their homeland to work like slaves in America?"

"As bad as these illegal immigrants have it in America, it's a thousand times better than what they have back in China," Ping said.

"Okay. Say I buy that for a minute," Johnny said. "But this fellow Housie, what's the deal with him?"

"Housie is a revered businessman in Chinatown," Ping said. "He runs an import/export business. Housie puts most of his profits back into the community. He funds the soup kitchen almost entirely by himself."

"And the envelope you gave him?"

"My humble contribution to the cause. Other Chinese business people contribute, too. When they can. We take care of our own."

"You mean, unlike the Italians," Johnny said.

Ping shrugged and said, "If the shoe fits."

"It fits alright," Johnny said. "The Italian mobsters in Little

Italy would run over their mothers if it put cash into their pockets. But truthfully, how many illegal Chinese immigrants do you think live right here in Chinatown?

"You're not working for immigration, are you?" Ping said.

"No. I have much more important things to do," Johnny said. "Like catching the real bad guys."

Before Ping could reply, three teenage Chinese gang members rushed through the front door of the restaurant; firing automatic weapons. They sprayed the floor and ceiling with gunfire; not particularly caring who or what they hit.

The restaurant was in absolute chaos. Patrons were screaming. Some were hit with the gunfire, while others dove to the floor under the tables.

As a waiter was hit while running back towards the kitchen, a young Chinese couple ran past the gunmen and fled out the front door.

Johnny pulled Ping to the ground, and her Christian Dior sunglasses flew off her face.

Johnny's cheek was nicked by either a bullet, or flying debris, and a small drop of blood ran down the side of his face.

Johnny overturned the table, using it as a shield, and he pulled out a gun from his shoulder holster. Johnny returned fire, and two of the gunman dropped to the floor, unconscious and possibly dead. Johnny then shot the third gunman in the foot. The third gunman screamed in pain. He did an about-face and quickly limped out the front door.

Johnny said to Ping, "Stay right here! Don't move!"

Ping pulled out her cellphone and said, "I'll call 911."

Johnny jumped to his feet. His gun leading the way, he pushed past terrified patrons and dashed out the front door.

Outside, he scanned in both directions through the thick lunchtime crowd. In seconds, Johnny spotted the third gunman limping into a car. The car sped away north on the Bowery, and past the Manhattan Bridge before Johnny could do anything.

Totally pissed off, Johnny holstered his gun and sprinted back into the restaurant.
He rushed back to Ping.

"Are you okay?" he said.

Ping examined her broken sunglasses, and then she said, "I'm fine. Just a little pissed off. These sunglasses cost me a mint."

"Do you know why anyone would want to kill you?" Johnny said.

"Kill me?" Ping said. "Are you crazy? They were shooting at *you*!"

"That's insane!" Johnny said. "Why would Chinese gangsters want to kill a New York City policeman? That makes no sense."

Ping wiped the blood off Johnny's cheek with a napkin. Then, she said, "It made sense to somebody."

Four cops and two paramedics rushed through the front door. As they assessed the situation, Johnny said to Ping, "We should have gone to Forlini's for lunch instead."

Ping stared at her broken sunglasses and said, "From your lips to God's ears."

Chapter Nine

Pete Grasso, his wife Rita, and his children Paulie and Lisa chowed down on spaghetti and meatballs at the dining room table.

Johnny entered the room; a bandage taped to his cheek. He removed his holstered gun and put it on the credenza. Then, he took a seat at the table and commenced eating.

"What happened to your cheek?" Rita said.

"A little scratch," Johnny said. "I was eating lunch in a Chinese dive in Chinatown, and some punks came in shooting."

"I told you!" Pete said. "That's why we moved to Brooklyn in the first place! The Chinks are shooting up the streets like cowboys!"

"I saw something about that on the Five O'clock News," Lisa

said. "Were you the cop who killed the two Chinese gangsters?"

Johnny stuffed a meatball in his mouth, and he said while chewing, "Just call me Johnny Deadeye."

"I saw that on TV, too," Paulie said. "One Chink got away, didn't he?"

"Yeah, but he's not getting around too good," Johnny said. "I shot him in the foot."

Rita grabbed her head with both hands and screamed, "Oh my God! My son gets shot just eating lunch in Chinatown! What's this world coming to?"

"I'm not sure it was an accident," Johnny said. "I was eating with Ping. She thinks I was the intended target."

"Why you?" Paulie said. "Why not her? Why not some other Chink in the joint?"

"I don't know. Maybe you could tell me," Johnny said.

"Me? I don't know nothing," Paulie said.

Johnny turned to his brother and said, "Did you hear about the early-morning shooting on Canal Street? Three Chinese gangbangers got blasted. And according to an eyewitness, the three shooters were white."

Paulie put a forkful of spaghetti into his yap. While chewing, he said, "I don't know nothing about it."

"Whatever," Johnny said.

Pete held his stomach, and he said to his wife, "Rita, honey, could you get me some Alka Seltzer. All this talk of people getting shot is giving me agita."

Ah Kay, Xin Lin, and Duk Tang sat at a table in their favorite Pell Street Chinese coffee shop; sipping cognac.

"So, what's this I hear about an Italian social club going up in flames?" Duk said.

"Like the Towering Inferno," Ah Kay said.

"The Greasers were hit so hard, olive oil was flowing in the streets," Xin Lin said.

"Word is that one of the Italians outside saw the person who threw the bomb," Duk said.

"So what?" Ah Kay said. "We outnumber the Italians 10-1 in Chinatown. If it comes down to an all-out war, we'll kick their

Guinea asses all the way back to the boot of Italy."

Duk stood and smacked Ah Kay's face. Then, he said, "And who gave the order to shoot the cop in broad daylight in Chinatown? That was damn stupid! It was all over the news on television and in the newspapers!"

"That cop's brother killed three of my best men," Ah Kay said. "That was my way of sending a message."

"Killing a cop sends a message alright," Duk said. "It shows the world how stupid you are."

"Maybe I should have confirmed it with you first," Ah Kay said.

"Damn right, you should have," Duk said. "Customers were shot. One waiter's dead. Where did you get these shooters from? The School For the Blind?"

"It was an initiation into our gang," Ah Kay said. "They failed the test. Two are dead, and the other one is injured."

"I'll make sure the injured boy is taken care of, too," Xin Lin said. "We have to tie up all the loose ends."

Duk took a sip of Cognac and said, "Right now, it looks like a coincidence the cop was in the Chinese restaurant during the shooting. If the New York City police department finds out the truth, it puts all our businesses in jeopardy."

"We'll ask our contact in the Fifth Precinct what the word is on the streets about the shooting," Xin Lin said.

"Still, the damage is done, as far as our neighborhood being safe for tourists," Duk said. "And that's got to hurt the Italian businesses, too. More than ours."

"Fuck the Italians," Ah Kay said. "I say we take out those fucking Greasers. Chinatown is our neighborhood now."

"Don't be so quick," Duk said. "Don Vito is not stupid. But I'm damn sure he's angry. And I'm angry, too."

Duk stood up. He cursed in Chinese, and then he threw his cognac glass against the wall.   Glass shattered in all directions.

It was a clear Sunday morning, and bright sunshine beat down from the cloudless sky in the Central Park softball field, as a brisk wind kicked up the infield sand.

While men and women played softball together in a mixed league, three men sat alone in the raised metal stands. One man was Carlo, and another was his boss, Vito Paisano; Johnny's and Paulie's uncle and their mother Rita's brother. Vito smoked a huge cigar, and he blew the smoke over his head in large circles.

Vito's bodyguard, Philly Guns, his right arm in a sling, sat two rows behind them. A bandage was taped to his forehead.

Vito turned and said to Carlo, "So, where were you when the lights went out?"

"We had a blackout?" Carlo said.

"No, moron," Vito said. "When our social club got bombed; where were you?"

"I was in the back room with your nephew, Paulie," Carlo said.

"And then?"

"I was knocked out cold. The next thing I knew, Paulie was dragging me out the back door."

"You say that you want a bump up to captain," Vito said. "But being a captain has certain responsibilities." Vito took a puff on his cigar, and then he continued, "You should have gone back in and tried to save people. Get them the fuck outta there!"

"Like I said, I was knocked out cold," Carlo said. "I wasn't thinking straight at the time."

"Good thing Sammy the Hook was strolling by," Vito said. "He called 911 from his cell. Then, he went inside and started pulling people out. Like the firemen did on 9/11."

Vito pointed his thumb back at Philly Guns and said, "Sammy the Hook saved my man Philly Guns and a half-a-dozen other men."

"Well, if I had all my senses, I would have done the same thing Sammy the Hook did," Carlo said.

"Maybe. Now, let's backtrack a little," Carlo said. "Sammy the Hook saw the people who threw the bomb. He said they were two Chinese gang members; those two mean motherfuckers always out in the streets terrorizing people. What's their names?"

"Chinamen bastards," Carlo said.

"No," Vito said. "I want their actual names!"

"I think I know who you mean," Carlo said. "Ah-something is one of them. I can't remember the other one's name."

"Do you know of any possible reason why Chinese gang members would want to torch our club?" Vito said.

"Not off the top of my head," Carlo said.

Vito puffed his cigar, turned to Philly Guns and said, "Not off the top of his head, he said."

"Don Vito, you gotta understand," Carlo said. "These Chinks are like animals. They enjoy doing stuff like that."

Vito raised his voice and said, "Don't call them Chinks! That's not nice! They're Chinese people!"

"Sorry," Carlo said. "But Chinese gang members kill just for the fun of it. They don't even need a reason."

Vito turned to Philly Guns. He shook his head and said, "They don't need a reason, he said."

"They're not like us Italians," Carlo said. "We only do things like that when it is absolutely necessary."

Vito stood and hovered menacingly over Carlo. Then he said, "Then tell me why it was absolutely fuckin' necessary for my nephew Paulie and two of his fuckin' jerkoff friends to whack three Chinese gang members on Canal Street the other fucking' night."

"Paulie?" Carlo said. "Nah, Paulie wouldn't do a thing like that without permission."

Vito sat back down and said, "Oh, he wouldn't, would he? And, to make it worse, in retaliation, the Chinese then came after Paulie's brother, my other nephew Johnny, who just happens to be a fuckin' New York City police detective."

"Nah. The way I heard it, those Chinks were after some Chink broad who was having lunch with your nephew the cop," Carlo said.

"Hey, what did I just tell you?" Vito said. "They're Chinese people! Not Chinks!"

"Sorry. Chinese. Not Chinks," Carlo said.

Vito pointed his cigar at Carlo and said, "Don't do it again."

Carlo put his head down in shame and said, "I won't. Promise."

"Look, I don't need all this aggravation," Vito said. "All I'm trying to do is find out what the fuck is going on in my own fuckin' neighborhood. And I don't want any trouble with the Chinese people. We're all in this together."

"I'll look into it," Carlo said. "I'll find out what's going on."

"You do that," Vito said. He waved his hand in disgust, and then he said to Carlo, "Now, get the fuck out of here."

Carlo stood, and without saying another word, he tottered down the steps of the metal stands and disappeared down the tree-lined road towards the park's exit.

With Carlo gone, Philly Guns hopped down the steps and sat next to Vito.

"Lyin' cocksucker," Philly Guns said. "He left me there to die. I should rip his heart out and feed it to the dogs."

"Hey! I should smack you in the face for talking about another made guy like that," Vito said.

"Sorry," Philly Guns said. "I was just talking to myself."

"I wish *I* was just talking to myself," Vito said. "I'd have a better conversation with myself than I would with any of you mooks."

"What's a mook?" Philly Guns said.

"Never mind," Vito said.

Vito stood, and Philly Guns did the same.

"Let's go," Carlo said. "If we shake a leg we can make the 12:20 Mass at Most Precious Blood."

Both men hopped quickly down the raised metal stands and headed out of the park.

Chapter Ten

The Chinese Bar on Bayard Street was packed with Chinese gangsters and their Chinese girlfriends. The gangsters wore black leather jackets and tight jeans. Their girlfriends wore tight skirts and low-cut blouses. All the girlfriends had spiky hairdos. Some had red hair, some had pink hair, and others had green hair; a regular kaleidoscope of feminine manes.

As loud chatter and laughter reverberated throughout the bar, on the stage in the back, a drunken Chinese man belted out off-key American karaoke with a Chinese accent.

Ah Kay sat at a table in the back near the stage. He was snorting coke like it was legal, along with his Chinese moll, Lois, who was wearing a tight black skirt that looked like it was painted on. Lois' hair was spiky pink, and a gun was stuffed into her skirt by her hip, barely hidden by her open red leather jacket.

Norman entered the bar, and he scanned the interior. He spotted Ah Kay's table, and he sauntered over. As Ah Kay snorted coke through a straw, Norman stopped and hovered over him.

Ah Kay looked up. He spotted Norman and said, "Hawaii Five-O is in the house." He offered the straw to Norman and said, "Care to indulge."

"No thanks," Norman said. "I'm still working."

Ah Kay pointed to Lois and said, "This is my girl, Lois."

Norman bent down until he was eye to eye with Lois. Then, he said, "You might want to zip up your jacket? The whole world can see that you've got a gun."

Lois pulled out a joint, and stuck it between her pouting lips. Then, she said, not too nicely, "Fuck off!"

"That's actually my gun," Ah Kay said to Norman. "My little lady always holds it for me. Just in case."

"I already knew that," Norman said. "This bitch is far from little, and not even close to being a lady."

Lois stared at Norman and said, "Stop taking those big nigger dicks up your ass. It's fuckin' up your mouth."

Norman leaned both hands on the table, and he said to Ah Kay, "Let's get to it. You're wasting my time."

Ah Kay handed Norman an envelope and said, "You know what you have to do. We want it done tonight."

Norman stuffed the envelope into his inside jacket pocket and said, "And stop snorting that garbage. It's making you stupid. And you're stupid enough to start with."

Norman made an about face and exited the bar.

An hour later, Norman, with Johnny sitting next to him, careened his unmarked police car through Chinatown. He handed Johnny an envelope and said, "That's your monthly cut from the Dukman."

Johnny put the envelope into his inside jacket pocket and said, "Thanks. I could use the cash."

"But we have one little favor to do," Norman said.

"I've got a feeling I'm not going to like this," Johnny said.

"Relax. Everything's going to be fine."

"I hate it when people tell me to relax."

"So relax, will ya?"

"Moron," Johnny said.

Minutes later, Norman parked the unmarked car on the corner of Pell and Doyers Street.

"What's going on?" Johnny said.

"We have to wait," Norman said.

Norman pulled an iPod out of his pocket. He clipped it to his belt and inserted the earplugs into his ears.

"What the heck are you doing?" Johnny said.

"Listening to Louie Prima," Norman said.

He started singing in Italian, *"C' 'NA LUNA MEZZ'U MARE MAMMA MIA M'A MARITARE."*

"You a real retard," Johnny said. "You really think you're Italian, don't you?"

Ten minutes later, a lone Chinese gangster exited a Chinese restaurant on Pell Street, and he limped down the deserted street."

Norman, the earplugs still in his ears, spotted the gangster; as did Johnny.

"Hey! That's the guy I shot in the foot!" Johnny said.

Norman removed the earplugs and put the iPod into his pocket.

"Let's see where he goes," Norman said.

The Chinese gangster passed the unmarked car and turned onto Doyers Street; a narrow lane shaped like an L. Norman slowly followed him.

Then, he stopped the car and put it into park.

"Let's go!" Norman said.

Norman bolted out of the car, and he sprinted after the Chinese gangster. Johnny jumped out of the car, and he raced after

Norman. Before the Chinese gangster could reach the corner of Chatham Square, Norman grabbed him by the collar.

The Chinese gangster turned around and said, "Hey! What the fuck?"

"Shut the fuck up," Norman said.

Then, Norman pushed the Chinese gangster into a dilapidated tenement.

Johnny looked both ways, and he saw nobody. Then, he followed Norman into the tenement.

Norman pushed the Chinese gangster past the stairs and into a small alcove behind the stairs.

"Stupid fuck," Norman said.

He began pummeling the Chinese gangster, with lefts and rights to the face and stomach. The Chinese gangster toppled to the floor and laid in a fetal position; blood dripping from his mouth.

Norman then punched and kicked the Chinese gangster repeatedly; like a madman.

"You fucked up big-time, pal!" Norman said.

The Chinese gangster sat up and spat into Norman's face.

"Fuck you," he said.

Norman pulled out his gun, and he pistol-whipped the Chinese gangster.

Just then, Johnny rushed into the tenement, and he pulled Norman off the Chinese gangster.

"Stop! Before you kill the guy!" Johnny said.

Norman stood up straight and told Johnny, "Okay. Check outside. Make sure the coast is clear."

"Alright," Johnny said. "Now, be cool."

Johnny turned and hurried towards the front door. But before he got there, he heard two loud gunshots. He turned around, and Norman rushed into Johnny. Then, he slipped his gun back into its holster.

"Let's move!" Norman said.

"What the hell did you just do?" Johnny said.

"The bastard spit in my face!" Norman said.

Johnny grabbed Norman around the throat with both hands and said, "So you fuckin' shoot him, you stupid bastard?"

Norman yanked Johnny's hands off his throat.

"It's too late now. He's dead," Norman said. "Let's get the

hell out of here!"

The two detectives dashed out of the tenement and jumped into their car; Norman again behind the wheel. Norman started the car and stepped on the gas, hard, and the car screeched away from the curb.

"You maniac bastard!" Johnny said. "What the hell's wrong with you?"

Norman, like he hadn't a care in the world, said to Johnny. "How about a little ride on the Staten Island Ferry?"

"You're crazy! You stupid Chinaman bastard!" Johnny said. "You just killed a guy."

Norman glanced at his wristwatch and said, "If we hurry, we can make the 4:30 am ferry."

"What's with the freakin' ferry?" Johnny said. "We've got big-time problems on our hands."

"I just love those ferry franks," Norman said. "They're better than Nathan's."

Johnny shook his head and said, "You're a fucking idiot."

Ten minutes later, Norman parked the unmarked car next to a fire hydrant in front of the Staten Island Ferry Terminal. Norman and Johnny exited the car.

"Quick. Let's split. It's almost 4:30," Norman said.

"But you parked by a hydrant," Johnny said.

"So what?" Norman said. "I'm a cop."

The two plainclothes cops dashed into the Staten Island Ferry Terminal.

Thirty minutes later, as a glimmer of light peeked through the sky, Johnny and Norman watched as the Staten Island Ferry glided past the Statue of Liberty.

They were standing on the bottom level of the ferry, the outside section in the back of the ferry. Norman had earplugs in his ears and an iPod clipped to his belt. He munched on a hot dog and washed it down with a gulp of soda from a huge Styrofoam container.

Norman took the earplugs out of his ears, and he said to Johnny, "Great franks. How come you're not eating?"

"I lost my appetite," Johnny said.

"Hey. Remember when they used to allow cars on the ferry?" Norman said.

"Yeah."

"They banned cars on the ferry after some jerk drove his car off the ferry into the water. Remember?"

"I remember."

"The fuckin' guy was a ferry employee, too," Norman said. "What a dickhead."

Norman finished his soda. He turned facing the water, and then he glanced towards the inside of the ferry.

No one was in sight.

Norman took the murder gun out of his pocket. He snapped the lid off the Styrofoam container, put the gun into the container, and put the lid back on the container. Then, he leaned over the railing and dropped the container into the water. The container bobbed for a second, and then it disappeared into the deep.

Johnny leaned over the railing and said, "What the fuck?"

"That gun was a throwaway. Untraceable," Norman said. "But I'm not taking any chances."

"Why in God's name did you kill that guy?" Johnny said. "He wasn't resisting arrest."

"I didn't plan on making an arrest," Norman said. "Those weren't my orders."

"From who?"

"What difference does it make? There's one less punk killer on the streets of Chinatown. And that's not a bad thing."

"He was one of the shooters in the restaurant," Johnny said. "We could have put him in prison for a very long time."

"For what reason?" Norman said. "That would have been a waste of taxpayer money. And that's not what we were getting paid for anyway."

"That's bullshit!" Johnny said. "I was getting paid to look the other way while the Chinese gangs ran a little gambling. The Italians pay us, too, to do the same thing for them. I was not paid to be an accessory to murder."

"If you take money from those Chinese gangs, you do what they tell you to do. Period," Norman said

Johnny jutted his nose inches from Norman's face and said, "And no more fuckin' surprises! You hear me!? You stepped way out of bounds on this one!"

"What are you worried about?" Norman said. "We just got

away with murder."

"We did what!" Johnny said. "Do you have a roach in your pocket or something? I had nothing to do with this."

Norman pulled out half-a-joint and said, "Yeah. I have a roach. Got a match?"

Johnny leaned on the railing facing the water and said, "You're a sick motherfucker. The way things have washed, whether I like it or not, I'm an accomplice to a fuckin' murder. And you, you fuck, were responsible for getting me into this mess."

Norman put the joint back into his pocket and said, "Don't worry. Nobody's going to miss that prick."

Johnny cradled his head in his hands and said, "I just wish this night was over."

"I need another frank," Norman said. "Want one?"

"I just hope that gun doesn't wash up anywhere," Johnny said.

"Wash up where?" Norman said. "The Atlantic Ocean swallowed up the evidence. There must be a million guns in the water here."

"Yeah. You're right," Johnny said. "I'm just freaked out. Fuckin' murderers. That's what we are. You pulled the trigger, but I'm just as guilty as you are for not arresting you on the spot."

"Whatever," Norman said. "It's dog time. Best dogs in town. Better than Katz's Deli. Sure you don't want one?"

"Fuck you and your hot dogs," Johnny said.

Norman shrugged. He turned and headed inside the ferry towards the hot dog counter.

Two hours later, Johnny entered the back of Transfiguration Church at 29 Mott Street in the heart of Chinatown.

Mass has already started, and up front at the altar, a priest, aided by two altar boys, said Mass. The priest's Latin chanting reverberated throughout the church.

The first two front pews were filled with old Chinese and Italian women dressed in black and wearing black kerchiefs over their heads. A handful of other parishioners dotted the other pews.

Johnny knelt in the last pew in the back of the church and started praying.

Finished, Johnny made the sign of the cross. He stood and headed for the back door of the church.

Johnny stopped at the poor box. From his inside jacket pocket, he took out the envelope Norman had given him, and he dropped it into the poor box.

Johnny dipped his hand in the holy water, and he genuflected, as he made the sign of the cross.

Then, he exited the church.

Chapter Eleven

Ping, wearing a white apron, stood behind the counter at the Chinatown soup kitchen and doled out portions of Chinese food to a queue of Chinese women.

Norman entered the soup kitchen. He grabbed a tray and stood in line. When Norman reached where Ping was standing, he snuck her an envelope.

Ping slipped the envelope into her apron pocket. Then, she spooned food onto a dish and placed the dish on Norman's tray.

Norman nodded to Ping. Carrying his tray of food, he walked past the counter, and he took a seat at an empty table.

An intoxicated man and woman entered Jimmy's Corner, a boxing-oriented dive located on 44th Street, fifty feet east of Times Square. They grabbed the first two seats by the front door; the only seats available in the entire place.

Jimmy's Corner was a long narrow bar with several tables in the back. The lights were dim, the walls were filled with boxing photos, and the jukebox blared Motown.

Black and white hookers and pimps mingled two-deep at the bar, amongst tourists from every city and country known to man. A few regulars that worked in the neighborhood rounded out the clientele, and everybody was having a grand old time.

The bartender/owner, Jimmy Glenn, was a large black man, with droopy eyes and a scowl on his face. He was arguing with a well-dressed white drunk sitting at the bar.

"I'm telling you, Muhammad Ali was the greatest," Jimmy said.

Ironically, Ali's autographed photo was planted directly on the wall behind him.

The drunk held on to his drink tightly, lest it fell and spilt the contents. He said,
"Rocky Marciano would have kicked Ali's black butt back to Africa."

"Ali was born in Louisville, Kentucky," Jimmy said.

"Same fucking thing," the drunk said.

Jimmy took the drink away from the drunk and said. "That's it for you. You've had enough."

"Hey man, that ain't right," the drunk said.

"Don't worry. I even call Uber for you and put it on my account," Jimmy said.

"Suppose I live in Connecticut?" the drunk said.

"Then, you're walking," Jimmy said. "Or the Uber can take you to Grand Central to catch the train."

"Fuck it," the drunk said. "I live downtown in the East Village. I'll take the subway."

He stood up and staggered to and out the front door.

Johnny and his brother Paulie sat at a small table in the back, both a little in the bag themselves.

"Only five bucks for a Dewars and soda," Paulie said. "I can't see how they stay in business."

"Look around you," Johnny said. "This place is packed like this every night. Sometimes you can't even get in the front door."

"Yeah. Someone once said, 'The joint is so crowded, nobody goes there anymore,'" Paulie said.

"That was Yogi Berra," Johnny said. "He also said, 'When you come to a fork in the road; take it.'"

"It's amazing that in this bar a 16-ounce tap beer is only three bucks," Paulie said. "That's 1970s uptown prices."

Johnny took a sip of his drink and said. "Well, little brother, you really screwed up big time this time. Because of what you did on Canal Street, I now have the Chinese gangs up my fucking ass. How could you do this to me?"

"I'm sorry," Paulie said. "I got in deep, gambling, and I figured this was my chance to climb out of my hole."

"What are you talking about?" Johnny said.

"With my cut from the Snakehead's smuggling operation, I could have paid all my debts," Paulie said. "Then, I would have been free and clear."

"You asked the Chinese gangs for a cut of their Snakehead business?" Johnny said.

"I didn't. Carlo did," Paulie said. "But it was basically my idea. And the Chinks basically told us to go fuck ourselves. I was there at the sit-down."

"Who else was there?"

"Me and Carlo. And Duk Tang and his flunkey, Ah Kay."

"And Uncle Vito said this was okay?"

"I didn't talk to Uncle Vito," Paulie said. "He's the top guy. You don't do things that way in the mob. You use the chain of command. So, I went to my boss Carlo. But I don't think he cleared it with Uncle Vito."

"Chain of command, my ass," Johnny said. "Vito's your uncle. He's not going to hold you to stupid bullshit like the so-called chain of command."

"Look, Carlo's my boss," Paulie said. "In this life, you do whatever your boss tells you to do. No questions asked. And you don't go over his head. Ever."

"Bullshit," Johnny said. "Uncle Vito is family. He's our blood; our mother's brother. Of course, you can talk to him directly without going through that greedy fuck Carlo."

"I don't know," Paulie said. "That doesn't sound right to me."

Johnny massaged his temples with both hands, and then he said, "Well, I know what I have to do now."

"What? What do you have to do?"

"Drink your drink," Johnny said. "I'm still thinking."

While a Chinese prostitute sat on the bed, Norman got dressed in a slimy room in a fleabag Manhattan Hotel.

The Chinese prostitute, wearing only bra and panties, counted the money Norman had just given her.

"Hey, mister! You're a hundred dollars short!" she said. "We agreed on two hundred, not one hundred dollars!"

Norman took out his wallet and flashed his police shield. Then, he said, "You're lucky you're getting paid at all. And you're lucky I don't pull you in."

"Typical cop," she said. "You guys always want something for nothing. Even pussy."

She stuffed the money inside her bra. Then, she jumped off the bed and started dressing; with her back to Norman.

From his pants pocket, Norman pulled out a .22 caliber pistol with a silencer attached to its muzzle. Then, he shot the Chinese prostitute twice in the back of the head. The gunshots were so muffled, it sounded like someone had just popped two small balloons.

She fell flat onto her face.

Norman paced to where she lay. He turned over her body. Her dead eyes were wide open, and blood spilled from the back of her head, forming a large puddle on the floor.

Norman reached into her bra, removed the hundred dollars, and put the money into his pants pocket.

"Like I said before," Norman said. "That's one less whore the city has to worry about."

Norman slipped the gun back into his pants pocket. He put on his sports jacket and exited the hotel room.

Chapter Twelve

Housie sat at his desk in the back room of the Chinese food kitchen. Ping entered the room and handed Housie a white envelope. Housie opened the envelope and counted the money.

"It's a little short," Housie said. "Maybe Norman is holding out."

"That doesn't surprise me," Ping said. "But there's one sure way to find out."

"Be careful," Housie said. "Those Big Circle Boys are very bad people. They kill just for the fun of it."

Ping opened her purse and pulled out a gun. He showed it to Housie.

"I've been through too much in my life to let them stop me now," she said. "Don't forget, when I was just a child, they kidnapped me, raped me, and held me hostage until I escaped."

"At least you left one of them dead for revenge," Housie said.

"One wasn't enough," Ping said.

"Just be careful," Housie said.

"I will. Don't worry," Ping said. "I've got everything covered."

Ping turned around and exited the office.

Johnny entered an apartment in a dilapidated Chinatown tenement on Mott Street. He was greeted by two men; both wearing FBI identification tags on chains around their necks. The tall thin one was named Ralph Burns and the shorter stockier one was Bruce Howard

Howard said to Johnny, "Give me the envelope Norman gave to you. I need it as evidence."

"The envelope is gone," Johnny said.

"What do you mean it's gone?" Burns said.

"I put it in the poor box at Transfiguration Church," Johnny said.

Burns turned to Howard and said, "I wondered what he was doing in that church."

Howard turned to Johnny and said, "You expect us to believe a bullshit story like that?"

"I don't give a fuck what you believe," Johnny said. "The poor people need that money more than the government does. I call it my own redistribution of wealth. Ask Bernie Sanders what that means."

Burns said, "This has to go into my report. It won't look good for you."

"Who gives a fuck?" Johnny said. "Now, let's get going. I don't have all fucking day."

Johnny took off his Rolex wristwatch and handed it to

Howard. Howard took off the back of the Rolex, and using tweezers, he pulled out a tiny transmitter.

Howard handed the transmitter to Burns and said, "That transmitter is fried. No wonder we weren't getting anything."

Using tweezers again, Burns inserted a new transmitter into the Rolex. Then, he snapped shut the back of the watch.

Burns gave the watch back to Johnny and said, "Now, it's good to go. Don't fuck this up."

Johnny strapped the Rolex back on his wrist and said, "Wonderful. You guys are geniuses. You're not as stupid as everyone thinks you are."

Howard ignored the remark and said to Johnny, "Duk Tang is going to request a meeting with you and Norman soon. We already have enough on your partner to put him away for a long time. But we really want Duk Tang."

"So, be careful and don't fuck this up," Burns said.

"You said that already," Johnny said. "Look. Let's get one thing straight. I hate the fucking FBI. Do you know what FBI stands for?"

"Federal Bureau of Investigation," Howard said.

"No," Johnny said. "It stands for Famous ... But ... Incompetent."

"Very funny," Burns said.

"All you guys think you're like J. Edgar Hoover," Johnny said. "And he was an incompetent prick, too."

"You're an asshole," Howard said.

"Look, I only agreed to work with you jerks because my boss in A. I. D. is a stand-up guy," Johnny said. "It was against my better judgment, but he talked me into it. But the minute this investigation is over, I'm through with you two pieces of shit. You got it?"

Johnny turned around. He opened the apartment door, and he exited the room; slamming the door behind him.

Johnny, Paulie, and Pete Grasso sat at the dining room table in Pete's home in Brooklyn. Two bottles of red wine stood on the table in front of them.

"Pour me a glass, will ya," Pete said to Paulie. "I need to get drunk."

Paulie poured the wine and handed the glass to Pete, saying, "Just one glass. According to mom, your blood pressure is going through the roof."

"If you start keeping tabs on me, *you're* going through the roof," Pete said.

"What do you say, guys?" Johnny said. "Do you want to do pistols at fifty paces?"

The front doorbell rang. Pete got up from the table, walked to the front door, and opened it.

Vito entered, and he hugged Pete. Pete turned to his two sons and said, "My brother-in-law Vito graces our humble abode."

He took Vito's arm and said, "Come in and sit."

Johnny and Paulie took turns hugging Vito. Then, Vito sat at the head of the dining room table and said, "Where's the food? I'm starving."

Rita and Lisa entered the dining room, both wearing cooking aprons.

Vito stood to greet the two women.

Rita kissed Vito's cheek and said, "My handsome brother."

Vito hugged Rita and said, "You're as beautiful as ever."

Paulie leaned over and whispered to Johnny, "Get me a paddle. It's getting pretty deep in here."

Lisa hugged Uncle Vito and kissed his cheek. She said, "Uncle Vito. It's wonderful to see you."

Vito said to Lisa, "You're gorgeous, just like your mother."

Paulie said, under his breath, "More bullshit."

Rita turned to Paulie and said, "Hey! Watch your mouth. No cursing at the dining room table. Remember?"

Then, she said to Vito, "We have to get back into the kitchen. Lisa is helping me with the manicot."

After Rita and Lisa went back into the kitchen, Vito said to Pete, "It's about time you invited me to dinner. It's nice to be with my family. You should invite me here more often."

"Vito, we know how busy you are in Manhattan," Pete said. "We hate to bother you."

"Bother me? Nonsense," Vito said. "You're all the family I've got."

"A little wine, Uncle Vito?" Johnny said.

"Sure. Is that a Chianti?" Vito said

"Bolla Bardolino. The best," Johnny said.

Johnny poured his uncle a glass of Bolla.

"I prefer Corvo myself," Paulie said.

"Then go buy some Corvo!" Peter said. "You've gotta spring for some cash once in a while. You're as tight as a clam's ass."

"I think Paulie has been springing a little bit too much lately," Vito said. "The springs are coming out of his brain.

"I got a feeling I don't want to hear this," Johnny said.

Vito leaned across the table, and Paulie leaned towards him. Their faces sat less than six inches apart.

Vito whispered to Paulie, "What the hell were you thinking? You know, that thing there on Canal Street near the Holland Tunnel." He pinched Paulie's cheek and said, "What are you? A cowboy or somethin'?"

Paulie leaned back and said, "Uncle Vito, you've got to believe me. That was not my call."

"But it was your original idea, wasn't it?" Vito said.

"Yeah, it was," Paulie said. "I had this idea about extorting money from the Chinks. I ran it past Carlo, who's my boss, and he liked the idea. I figured he ran it past you and got your permission."

"They're Chinese people," Vito said. "Don't call them Chinks."

"Okay," Paulie said. "But these Chinese gangs are making tons of money smuggling Chinese human cargo from China into the United States. For as much as fifty large a head."

"So, what does that have to do with us?" Vito said.

"I figured it's our streets they're crowding with thousands of fuckin' Chink ..."

"Don't say it," Vito said.

"Chinese people."

"That's better."

"So, why shouldn't we get our cut?" Paulie said.

"Number one, that's for me to decide," Vito said. "Number two, considering number one, why didn't you just come to me in the first place?"

"I followed the chain of command," Paulie said. "I went to Carlo. He's my boss. Those are the rules, ain't they?"

"Yes, normally, those are the rules," Vito said. "But you're my nephew. Fuck the rules!"

"Okay, fuck the rules."

"What happened next?"

Carlo called for a sitdown with Duk Tang," Paulie said. "I was there. The Dukman turned us down flat."

"This is the first time I'm hearing about this," Vito said.

"What? Carlo never told you about any of this?"

"Not a word. If he had, I would have turned *him* down flat. That's Chinese business. It's none of our affairs."

"Maybe Carlo didn't tell you because he wanted the money all for himself," Pete said.

"Could be," Vito said. "You can never tell what a prick like Carlo is thinking."

"I'd like to get my hands around Carlo's neck," Paulie said.

"Calm down, Paulie," Vito said. "Carlo's a made-guy. You can't talk about him like that. Especially in front of me. Those are the rules, too."

Vito took a sip of wine and said, "Until now. In fact, that's one of the reasons I'm here. Besides dining with my wonderful family."

"I think I know where this is heading," Johnny said. He stood up from the table and said, "Uncle Vito, I'm a cop. Do you want me to leave the room?"

"No, of course not. You're my nephew," Vito said, smiling. "You're not going to arrest me, are you?"

"No, of course not," Johnny said.

"Then sit down," Vito said. He pointed to the Rolex on Johnny's wrist and said, "I see you're not wearing the Rolex that I gave you. That's a different one. What did you do? Lose it?"

Johnny sat down and said, "I only wear that Rolex for special occasions."

"Smart boy," Vito said.

"Rolex watch? What's going on here?" Paulie said.

"Nothing," Vito said. "Mind your own business."

"Yeah. Mind your own business," Pete said to Paulie.

"Before the girls come back, I want to get this out of the way," Vito said.

"Someone's getting shot," Johnny said.

Vito reached across the table and held Paulie's two hands in his own two hands.

"You're getting into too much trouble," Vito said. "I need to keep an eye on you. And the best way to do that is to give you your button. You'll answer directly to me. Carlo will be completely out of the picture. What do you say?"

"I don't know what to say," Paulie said.

"You can say no, and there will be no hard feelings," Vito said. "You're still my nephew."

"I'm a little overwhelmed here," Paulie said. "Can I think it over?"

"Sure. Think it over," Vito said. "Take your time. But I have something you might want to do to make some easy dough. How much do you owe Carlo?"

"Fifty large."

"A man of honor always pays his debts," Vito said. "Maybe I can help you out."

"How?" Paulie said.

"Easy guys," Johnny said. "There's a cop sitting here."

"I'll tell you after dinner," Vito said to Paulie. "You come with me into the city. We'll talk."

Rita tramped into the room carrying a large tray of antipasto. She said, "Start with this, gentlemen. Lisa and I are still working on the manicot and the meatballs."

Then, she went back into the kitchen.

"Great! Let's dig in!" Pete said.

Johnny filled everyone's glass with wine.

Vito raised his glass and said, "To famiglia!"

Johnny, Paulie, and Pete lifted their glasses and said in unison, "To famiglia!"

Chapter Thirteen

As Ping sat behind her desk at the travel agency shuffling
paperwork, Johnny entered the room wearing his special Rolex

wristwatch.

"How about I take you out to lunch?" Johnny said. "I still owe you one from the time we almost got killed."

"I don't know," Ping said. "The last time you took me to lunch, I wound up with broken Christian Dior sunglasses."

"Don't worry," Johnny said, waving a large paper bag. "I know the perfect place."

Ten minutes later, Johnny and Ping sat on a park bench in Columbus Park across the street from the Criminal Courts Building. Both were chowing down on hot Italian sandwiches Johnny had purchased at Forlini's.

While cooing pidgins flocked throughout the park looking for food, clusters of people, both Chinese and non-Chinese, milled about. Behind Johnny and Ping, old Chinese women performed their daily Kung Foo exercises.

Johnny, holding a hot sandwich in one hand, said, "So, tell me, what do you really know about the Snakeheads?"

Ping took a bite of her sandwich. She chewed for a full twenty seconds, swallowed, and then she said. "Why would I know anything about Snakeheads?"

"Because I know you do," Johnny said. "I'm a detective. Remember? And detectives detect things."

"So, you know more about me than I thought," Ping said.

"Just a little," Johnny said.

Ping took another bite of her sandwich. This time she chewed even longed while Johnny waited for her answer.

"Well to start with, there are Snakeheads, and then there are the *Enren*," she finally said.

"Whoa! *Enren*?" Johnny said. "That sounds like a birth control foam."

"The Snakeheads you know all about already," Ping said. "If they are not paid on time, they do horrible things to the poor Chinese immigrants whom they smuggled into the United States."

"Sometimes they kill them," Johnny said. "I heard that the girls are often raped."

"Yes, that is true," Ping said. "Then, besides the Snakeheads, there are Chinese people, upstanding businessmen and businesswomen, who help poor Chinese people get into America."

"What exactly do you mean by help?" Johnny said.

"They help by bribing officials at the immigration checkpoints," Ping said. "Or by obtaining forged documents to get these poor Chinese people into America. Nobody gets hurt."

"That's still against the law," Johnny said.

"Whose law? Not our law!" Ping barked. "Our people are just trying to survive."

"Ok, I'll let that one pass," Johnny said. "But who pays for all this? The *Enren*?"

"Sometimes they do," Ping said. "Especially when the people being smuggled in don't have the money to pay for things like forged documents."

"Or bribes?"

"Or bribes."

"Forgive me if I think what you're telling me is Fantasy Land," Johnny said. "Or maybe something out of the *Twilight Zone*."

"Think what you like," Ping said. "But it's all true."

"All right, if you say so," Johnny said. "Now, tell me more about these *Enren*."

"The *Enren* are mostly well-to-do business people living in Chinatown," Ping said. "In addition to providing the planning and the routes, they give the illegal immigrants interest-free loans to cover the expenses they incur to enter and stay in the United States."

"Interest-free loans?" Johnny said. "That's a new concept in America."

"The loans usually originate in China," Ping said.

"Which was a Communist country," Johnny said.

"Which is still an oppressive country to the poor," Ping said.

"So, America is better for these people being smuggled in?" Johnny said. "Better than their homes in China."

"Much better."

"That's hard to believe."

"When the illegals get into America, the *Enren* find them jobs; either in restaurants or in sweatshops," Ping said.

"Where they work 80 hours a week for much less than minimum wage."

"The system isn't perfect," Ping said. "But I'm telling you, no matter how bad the jobs are the illegals get in America, it's a hundred times better than the life they have in China."

"But it must take them years to pay back these loans."

"Not really," Ping said. "Remember, the *Enren* make no money on this. The expenses may be five, ten thousand dollars. Tops. The illegals pay back the money they owe as fast as they can. And they always do. It's a matter of honor."

"Look, I see where you're coming from," Johnny said. "But these *Enren* are still breaking the laws here in America. You can't convince me otherwise."

"Who cares about the American laws?" Ping said. "These laws are applied arbitrarily anyway. The *Enren* feel they are doing nothing wrong. They feel they are performing a public service to the Chinese community. And the Chinese community agrees with them."

"I'd have a hard time getting that past my boss in the Fifth Precinct," Johnny said.

"People have to do what they have to do to survive. What's wrong with people striving for a better life?"

"Well, for one thing, these people can enter the country legally," Johnny said. "We have the mechanisms in place here in America for them to do just that. They have to fill out the proper forms and go through the proper channels. And wait a certain period of time."

"Oh please!" Ping screamed. "Since 9/11, the immigration movement in the United States has been at a standstill. American immigration officials think everyone's a terrorist."

"Turn around," Johnny said. He turned toward the southwest. "Look at the sky. What don't you see?"

Ping turned, too, and then she said, "I know. The World Trade Center. It's gone."

"That's right," Johnny said. "After 9/11, do you think the United States wants to make it easy for foreigners to come into this country? We just can't take that risk."

"I understand your point," Ping said. "And that's exactly why the *Enren* are needed. And that's why it's imperative to crack down on the Snakeheads who are extortionists, rapists, and murderers."

Johnny took a bite of his sandwich, and then he said, "Okay. Let me chew on that one for a little while."

An isolated truck was parked 100 yards from the public restrooms in a truck stop on the New Jersey Turnpike. The driver was asleep behind the wheel.

Suddenly, an old Plymouth police car, that had seen better days, parked next to the truck. Three men wearing Halloween masks exited the vehicle.

Hijacker No. 1 knocked on the truck driver's side window, while the other two trained pistols at the driver's door.

The driver awoke and rolled down the window.

Hijacker No. 1 put a gun into the truck driver's face and yelled, "**GET OUT OF THE FUCKING TRUCK! ... NOW! ... HANDS BEHIND YOUR HEAD!**"

The frightened truck driver exited the truck; his hands interlocked behind his head.

The hijackers tied the truck driver's hands behind his back with rope. Then, they slapped duct tape over his mouth to keep him quiet.

Hijacker No. 2 opened the driver's door of the old Plymouth, and he got behind the wheel.

Hijacker No. 1 opened the back door of the car, and he pushed the truck driver into the back seat. Then, he slipped into the back seat next to him.

Hijacker No. 3 jumped into the truck. He got behind the wheel and took off his mask.

It was Jimmy Ryan.

Jimmy put the truck in gear and drove onto the Jersey Turnpike heading south.

In the back seat of the old Plymouth, Hijacker No. 1 stuck his gun into the truck driver's ribs and said "No funny stuff, and you'll get out of this alive.

Hijacker No. 2 drove the car out of the truck stop and onto the Jersey Turnpike. A half-a-mile later, he pulled the car over to a secluded area on the side of the road.

Hijacker No. 1 got out of the back seat of the car, and he dragged the truck driver out of the back seat and onto the unpaved ground.

Hijacker No. 2 also exited the car. He patted down the truck driver and found the truck driver's wallet.

He pulled the truck driver's license out of the wallet, and he handed it to Hijacker No. 1.

Hijacker No. 1 peered at the truck driver's license and said, "Now we know where you live. Don't be a hero."

Hijacker No. 1 slipped the license into his own pants pocket, and then he told the truck driver, "Forget all about this. Or we'll come looking for you and your family."

The truck driver made muffled sounds that showed he understood.

Hijacker No. 1 put the wallet back into the truck driver's pants pocket.

Then, Hijacker No. 2 covered the truck driver's nose and mouth with a cloth soaked in ether.

In seconds, the truck driver lost consciousness and rolled onto his side.

The two hijackers dragged the truck driver behind a tree. They placed him in a sitting position and wrapped another rope around the truck driver and the tree. Hijacker No. 2 tied the loose ends of the rope behind the tree tightly with an intricate knot.

"He ain't going nowhere," Hijacker No. 2 said.

"Right. Let's split," Hijacker No. 1 said.

Hijacker No. 1 took off his mask.

It was Paulie Grasso.

Hijacker No. 2 took off his mask.

It was Billy the Polark.

"My Uncle Vito was right," Paulie said. "This score was a cinch."

Paulie and Billy the Polark got back into the car; Billy behind the wheel and Paulie in the passenger's seat.

Billy directed the old Plymouth back onto the Jersey Turnpike.

Chapter Fourteen

Norman drove his unmarked car east on Canal Street with Johnny sitting next to him.

"I just got a call on my cell," Norman said. "Duk Tang wants to meet us right away."

"What for?" Johnny said.

"Who knows? It will only take a minute."

"What if we get a police call?"

"Don't worry. I said this will be quick," Norman said.

"Okay. But let's stop at Forlini's first," Johnny said. "I've got to make a head stop."

Carlo stood on a Brooklyn Street corner and spoke into one of the last pay phones in modern civilization.

"Paulie, I've got good news for you," Carlo said. "Put on your best suit."

"What's this all about?" Paulie said.

"No questions," Carlo said. "I'll pick you up in an hour."

Then, he hung up the phone.

Johnny slipped into the men's room at Forlini's, and he was grateful it was empty. He went inside one of the two stalls and locked the stall door behind him.

He spoke softly into his Rolex wristwatch, saying, "This is John Grasso. Detective First Grade. New York City Police Department. And I'm consenting to record my conversation with Duk Tang, Detective Norman Wong, and others as yet unknown."

Johnny exited the stall and bellied up to the sink. He washed his face and hands. Then, he removed several paper towels from the towel dispenser and wiped his hands dry.

Johnny stared into the mirror and softly said, "It's Showtime."

Johnny straightened his tie. Then, he shrugged his shoulders, like a gangster in a 1930s movie and exited the bathroom.

A Lincoln Town Car pulled into the driveway at the Grasso residence in Brooklyn. Carlo got out of the front passenger's seat, and Philly Guns did the same from the driver's seat. His right arm was still in a sling.

Paulie sauntered out the front door of his house. He was wearing his best suit and a white silk shirt, with a tacky mob tie and a matching pocket handkerchief.

Carlo and Philly Guns took turns hugging Paulie and kissing

him on both cheeks.

"You look good, Paulie," Carlo said. "Today is your lucky day."

Paulie, as nervous as a long-tailed cat in a room filled with rocking chairs, said, "I hope you're right."

Carlo opened the front passenger's door, and Paulie slid into the front passenger's seat.

Philly Guns got behind the wheel, and Carlo jumped into the back seat.

Philly Guns turned the ignition key and the car hummed to life.

Paulie said to Philly Guns, "How can you drive with just one hand?"

"Very slowly and very carefully," Philly Guns said. "You got a problem with that?"

"No. Not at all," Paulie said.

"Hey, cut the chatter," Carlo said. "We've got some serious business to take care of."

Philly Guns glanced behind him. He put the car in reverse and backed out of the driveway. Then, he put the car into drive, and the car blended into traffic.

Ah Kay opened the front door of a Chinese Restaurant on Chatham Square. Xin Lin stood behind him.

Johnny and Norman entered, and Johnny closed the door behind him.

Ah Kay led the detectives to a side door. Xin Lin frisked both cops and removed their guns. Then he said, "Sorry, no guns allowed downstairs."

He opened the door to the basement and said, "After you."

Norman peeked down the darkened steps leading to the basement and said, "Looks like a fuckin' cave."

The two detectives headed down the steps, followed by Ah Kay and Xin Lin.

The basement room was dimly lit, and there was no furniture, except for a rectangular table set in the middle of the room; with two chairs facing two other chairs on either side of the table.

Duk Tang sat on one side of the rectangular table, and Ping

sat next to him.

Ping was wearing a black leather jacket and tight jeans; typical Chinese gangster/girlfriend – type attire. She was not wearing her usual black-rimmed Christian Dior glasses.

Johnny and Norman entered the room, followed by Ah Kay and Xin Lin.

When he saw who was present, Johnny said to Ping, "What are you doing here?"

"You'll find out soon enough," Ping said.

Duk Tang said to Johnny, "I see you know Sister Ping." He pointed to the two chairs opposite him and said, "Gentlemen, please be seated."

The two detectives sat opposite Duk Tang and Ping.

Ah Kay and Xin Lin stood menacingly behind them. Their arms were folded across their chests; like big-time bodyguards in a grade B movie.

"Would anyone like some tea?" Duk Tang said. "Or maybe some cognac?"

"No. We're good," Johnny said.

"Then, let's get down to business," Duk Tang said. "Detective Grasso, may I see your wristwatch?"

Johnny extended his arm to Duk Tang, exposing his bugged watch.

"It's a Rolex," Johnny said.

"That I can see," Duk Tang said. "Now, take it off and hand it to me."

Johnny took off the Rolex and handed it across the table to Duk Tang.

Ah Kay sauntered around the table, and Duk Tang gave Ah Kay the wristwatch.

Ah Kay dropped the wristwatch to the floor and stomped it into little pieces.

The transmitter was clearly visible inside the crushed Rolex.

"What the hell's going on here?" Norman said.

"In due time, Detective," Duk Tang said. "In due time."

Philly Guns parked the Lincoln Town Car next to a hydrant in front of an Italian social club in Bay Ridge, Brooklyn. Carlo, Philly Guns, and Paulie exited the car.

An Italian mobster with hair on his knuckles guarded the front door to the club. He was so tall and wide, he obscured the entire entrance.

Philly Guns handed the huge Italian mobster the keys to the Lincoln Town Car and said, "Take care of this for me. Will ya?"

"No problem, Philly," the Italian mobster said.

Carlo entered the club; followed by Paulie and Philly Guns.

Like before, Duk Tang and Ping still sat on one side of the rectangular table. And Johnny and Norman sat opposite them. Ah Kay and Xin Lin stood behind the detectives.

Duk Tang said to Norman, "Killing comes easy to you. Doesn't it, Norman?"

"I do my best," Norman said. "It's just a job. Like any other job."

"And because of your unmatched ruthlessness, you have been a very important chess piece in my organization," Duk Tang said.

"Like I said, I do my best," Norman said.

"However, it has come to my attention that you have spun out of control," Duk Tang said. "And now you have cost me money and much prestige; face, as we Chinese like to call it."

"Cost you money and prestige? How?" Norman said.

"You raped and killed a young Chinese prostitute in a hotel," Duk Tang said. "This young girl was under my protection, and now you have to pay for her loss."

"You're crazy!" Norman said. "I didn't kill your Chinese whore!"

"Sorry, but that's simply not true," Duk Tang said. "Since this young girl was one of mine, she was followed at all times. You were seen entering the hotel with her, and you were seen leaving alone." He nodded at Ah Kay and Xin Lin. Then, he said, "Right, gentlemen?"

Norman turned around. Ah Kay and Xin Lin both flashed him a wicked smile.

Norman stood up with his fists balled and said, "Fuck you! Fuck you all!"

Norman charged the two Chinese bodyguards.

Ah Kay pulled out a gun with a silencer attached to the muzzle, and he shot Norman twice in the chest. The gunshots sounded like air flying from a pea shooter.

Norman slumped to the floor.

Ah Kay fired twice more, and both shots blasted into Norman's head.

Norman's body wiggled; then he stopped moving.

He was as dead as a dodo bird.

Duk Tang said to Johnny, "And now you, Detective. What do you propose I should do with you?"

Carlo entered the Italian social club; followed by Paulie and Philly Guns. Vito stood at the entrance, facing the three men. He had a mountainous bodyguard on each side of him.

Vito pointed to a side door and said, "Welcome gentlemen. The meeting is in the basement."

Carlo tried to hug Vito, saying, "Don Vito."

Vito backed away and said, "Not this time, Carlo."

With his good hand, Philly Guns pulled out a gun from his jacket pocket. He aimed over Paulie's shoulder, and he shot Carlo twice in the back.

Paulie recoiled from the loud noise; his hands covering his ears.

Carlo fell to his knees and turned towards Philly Guns.

Philly Guns shot Carlo twice more in the chest, and Carlo fell onto his back.

Philly Guns leaned over Carlo, and put two more bullets into Carlo's head. Carlo fell to his side, quite dead.

Philly Guns spat on Carlo and said, "You rat bastard! You left me for dead!"

All through the shooting, Paulie just stood there; petrified.

Pointing to Carlo's dead body, Vito said to his two bodyguards, "Take this trash out back. There's a car waiting. Then, come back here and clean up this mess."

Paulie whipped out a handkerchief from his inside suit jacket pocket and wiped his brow.

"Damn. I didn't expect this," Paulie said.

Vito hugged his nephew and said, "You were worried? Do you think your Uncle Vito would do you any harm?" Then, he pointed to Philly Guns and said, "Meet your new captain."

Paulie hugged Philly Guns and said, "Congratulations, Philly."

"Same to you kid," Philly Guns said.

Vito's two bodyguards rolled open a tarp next to Carlo's body. They flipped Carlo's body onto the tarp; then folded the tarp around the body. Then, they dragged the body out the back door.

Vito motioned to the side door and said to Paulie, "Let's go downstairs. We have important business to attend to." Then, he turned to Philly Guns and said, "I have the needle to prick his finger. Did you bring the religious card and the matches."

Philly Guns tapped his breast pocket and said, "Right here, boss."

"Which saint's card did you bring?" Carlo said.

Philly Guns shrugged and said, "I dunno. St. Joseph, I think. Or maybe St. Peter. St. Jude? The saints all look the same to me anyway. They all have the same halos."

Vito shook his head in disgust and said, "Let's go downstairs. I need a fuckin' drink."

Chapter Fifteen

Norman's dead body still lay on the floor in the basement of the Chinese Restaurant. Johnny, his nerves frayed, sat at the rectangular table opposite Duk Tang and Ping. Ah Kay and Xin Lin stood menacingly behind him.

"So, I ask you again," Duk Tang said to Johnny. "What do you propose I should do with you?"

"I could use a little vacation," Johnny said. Then, he looked mean at Ping and said, "Hey, Sister Ping. Could you hook me up with a nice long trip to Hong Kong?"

"You are going on a nice long trip," Duk Tang said. "But not to Hong Kong."

"What do you mean?" Johnny said.

Duk Tang placed a portable iPod docking station on the table and inserted an iPod into it. Then, he pressed the "on" button.

Norman's voice came in loud and clear on tape. He said, *"What are you worried about? We got away with murder."*

Johnny said on the tape, *"Yeah. You're right. Fuckin' murderers. That's what we are. I wish this night was over. I just hope that gun doesn't wash up somewhere."*

Norman's voice said, *"That gun was a throwaway. Untraceable. Don't worry. The ocean swallowed up the evidence."*

"Yeah. You're right. I'm just freaked out." Johnny's voice said.

Duk Tang turned off the iPod and said, "Sounds like an airtight case to me. Enough for a long trip to the penitentiary."

Johnny stood up and screamed, "That recording was doctored! Everything was switched around and taken out of context."

"Tell that to the FBI," Duk Tang said.

Johnny pushed back hard with his chair, knocking both Ah Kay and Xin Lin backwards. Ah Kay pulled out his gun and pointed it at Johnny.

Suddenly, Ping jumped to her feet. She pulled out a gun, and she shot a very shocked Xin Lin and Ah Kay each twice in the chest. Both toppled onto their backs; very dead.

Duk Tang sprinted, as fast as his fat body could take him, toward the stairs. But Ping tackled him before he got there. Then, she pulled Duk Tang to his feet.

Ping yanked a set of handcuffs from inside her leather jacket, and she cuffed Duk Tang's hands behind his back.

Suddenly, four FBI Swat Team members, aiming assault rifles, stormed down the stairs. They were followed by FBI agents Ralph Burns and Bruce Howard. Ping handed Duk Tang over to the swat team, and the swat team pushed Duk Tang up the stairs.

Ping turned to Agents Burns and Howard and said, "Where were you guys? On spring break?"

"Sorry, Agent O'Reilly," Burns said. "We burst through the upstairs door as soon as we heard the first shots on the transmitter."

"Agent O'Reilly?" Johnny said.

Ping took her trademark Christian Dior eyeglasses out of the inside pocket of her black leather jacket and put them on.

"Agent Ping O'Reilly, actually," she said.

Johnny turned to the two FBI agents and said, "You guys said you heard the shots over my transmitter? That's impossible! They smashed my Rolex to pieces!"

Ping showed Johnny the Rolex watch on her wrist. Then, she said, "I have one of those doohickeys, too."

"My head is spinning here," Johnny said. "Could somebody please tell me what the fuck just happened?"

"I'll leave that up to Agent O'Reilly," Burns said. "You haven't been too nice to us lately."

"Not too nice?" Johnny said. "What did you want me to do? Take you guys to the senior prom?"

Howard pulled out his FBI badge and said to Johnny, "Remember? ... F ... B ... I ... Famous But Incompetent."

"I was just kidding, guys," Johnny said. "Just a little joke of mine."

"You can take your jokes and shove them," Burns said.

Ping grabbed Johnny's arm and said, "I'll explain every little detail; if you buy me dinner at Forlini's."

"Buy you dinner? You just saved my life!" Johnny said. "I'll buy you your own freakin' restaurant!"

"Dinner will suffice," Ping said.

"What about us? Don't we get dinner too?" Howard said.

"Sure," Johnny said. "There's a nice little Chinese joint on Chatham Square with dead ducks and chickens hanging in the window. But don't order the pork fried rice. In fact, I would stay away from the pork and chicken dishes altogether."

"Wiseguy," Burns said.

"Are either of you guys allergic to cats?" Johnny said.

Ping grabbed Johnny's arm and pulled him up the stairs before the FBI agents could answer.

Johnny and Ping sat at a table in the back room of Forlini's. They were the only customers in the establishment.

A busboy removed the soiled dinner dishes. A second busboy swept the crumbs off the table into a small dish.

A waiter brought over a tray containing a bottle of Chivas Regal, a bucket of ice, and two glasses. He placed the tray on the table.

"This is on Derek," the waiter said. Then, he exited the back room.

Johnny filled the two glasses with Chivas and a few rocks, and he handed a glass to Ping.

Johnny raised his glass and said, "Salute!"

Ping did the same, and they both downed the Chivas in one large swallow.

Johnny leaned back in his chair and said. "Well, we both had a wild ride today. Fill me in on the details that I obviously missed."

"Where should I start?" Ping said.

"How about at the beginning?" Johnny said.

"Ok," Ping said. "Years ago, when I was barely a teenager, the Snakeheads smuggled me into New York City."

"The Snakeheads," Johnny said. "Not the *Enren*?

"Yes. The Snakeheads," Ping said. "There were no *Enren* at the time."

Ping poured them each another glass of Chivas. Then, she said, "My parents died when I was young. So, my uncles in China gave the Snakeheads a $10,000 down payment to smuggle me into America: The so-called Mountain of Gold."

"How much did your uncles owe the Snakeheads after you arrived in America?" Johnny said.

"Another $40,000," Ping said. "But my uncles couldn't pay. And with the money I was making working in the Chinese sweatshops, it would have taken me the rest of my life to settle the debt." She downed her Chivas and said, "Then one day, I escaped."

"What do you mean - escaped?" Johnny said.

"It's a long story," Ping said. "I'd rather keep that part a secret."

"Okay, I get it," Johnny said. "Don't ask. Don't tell. Sounds like the government's policy on gays in the military." He sipped his Chivas and said, "So, where did you go? You had no family here in America."

"I went straight to the police," Ping said. "I told them the truth about me being in the country illegally. I also told them about the Snakeheads. Instead of deporting me, they brought the FBI into the picture. And the FBI placed me in a nice foster home. The O'Reillys took good care of me for many years."

"Where are the O'Reillys now?" Johnny said.

"They both passed away," Ping said. "First my mother. She had a sudden massive heart attack. No warning, no nothing. I was devastated. My father died nine months later from a broken heart."

"Jesus, I'm sorry," Johnny said.

"The truth is, I have no family here in the United States," Ping said. "And there's very little I can remember about my relatives in China."

Housie entered the back room of the restaurant. He paced slowly to their table and kissed Ping's cheek.

Johnny stood. Housie bowed slightly, and then he shook Johnny's hand.

"Have a seat. Can I get you a drink?" Johnny said.

"Two fingers of that Chivas would be fine," Housie said.

Johnny snatched a glass from an adjoining table, and he poured Housie a short Chivas. Then, he slumped back into his chair.

Ping said to Housie, "I was just telling Johnny the details of how I arrived in America."

"Yes. Sister Ping went through some very hard times," Housie said. "But hard times make strong people."

Ping turned to Johnny and said, "Now, tell me about yourself. How long have you been working undercover for the FBI?"

"Not for the FBI; with the FBI," Johnny said. "Those guys are jerks."

Ping smiled and said, "Remember. I'm with the FBI, too."

"Right. But you're different," Johnny said. "Obviously, very different."

He took a sip of his scotch and said, "I started working undercover right after I was promoted to Detective. Internal Affairs contacted me about working in conjunction with the FBI to bring down the Chinese gangs."

"So, they partnered you with Norman Wong," Ping said. "Who was worse than most of the Chinese gang members."

"They figured Norman was up to something bad. But they wanted evidence linking him to more serious crimes," Johnny said. "We didn't realize how bad he had gone."

Housie stood and said, "Kids, I must leave you now. I have very important business to attend to."

Johnny stood and shook Housie's hand. Then, he said, "I guess I'll be seeing you around."

"Yes. God willing," Housie said.

Then, Housie said to Ping, "I came here tonight for a reason. Please, see me first thing tomorrow morning. We have more work to do."

"I'll be there with bells on," Ping said.

Housie bowed and said, "Goodbye to you both."

Then, he exited the dining room.

Johnny said to Ping, "I'll make believe I didn't hear that. How about I pick you up for lunch tomorrow?"

Ping stood and said, "Great. I'll meet you in my office at noon."

Johnny stood, and she kissed him on the cheek.

"I expect a little more than a peck on the cheek the next time," Johnny said.

"Okay," Ping said. "I'll take that under advisement."

Chapter 16

Housie sat behind his desk in the back of the Chinese soup kitchen; shuffling papers. There was a knock on his office door. Like a man with a bad back, he shuffled to the door, peeked through the peephole, and then he opened the door.

Ping entered; carrying a shopping bag. She kissed Housie on the cheek and said, "Good morning, dear sir."

Housie sat back at his desk, and he pointed to a chair on the opposite side of the desk.

"Please sit," Housie said. "Or as they like to say in America, 'Take a load off.'"

Housie reached into his desk drawer, and he removed a large manila envelope. He handed the envelope across the desk to Ping and said, "There's $30,000 in that envelope. I have three more people in China ready to escape. Spread the money around where it's needed. If you need more money, come back to me."

Ping put the manila envelope into her shopping bag and said,

"I have to check the flight schedules. I want to put the three people on three different flights. Just to be safe."

"You are doing good work, Sister Ping," Housie said. "The Chinese community is very proud of you. I was afraid you were going to be transferred by the FBI out of Chinatown."

"Me too," Ping said. "But I convinced my superiors that I can be more valuable here working in Chinatown than I can sitting behind a desk somewhere else."

"There's still the Chinese gangs to deal with," Housie said. "And the Tongs are presently deciding on Duk Tang's replacement."

"So, I was right," Ping said. "There is much more work for me to do here."

"And as always, be careful," Housie said.

"And as always, I will," she said.

Ping stood, and then she exited the room.

Ping sat behind her desk at her travel agency. On the desk was the manila envelope Housie had just given her.

Without knocking, Johnny entered Ping's office.

Seeing Johnny, Ping secretly slipped the manila envelope into her desk drawer.

"Are you hungry?" Johnny said.

"I'm famished," she said.

Johnny showed Ping a brown paper bag and said, "I bought two sandwiches at Forlini's. Meatball and chicken parm."

"I'll take the meatball," she said.

"Great," Johnny said. "I'll take the chicken parm."

Johnny and Ping strolled arm in arm through the dense lunchtime crowd on Bayard Street. Johnny carried the paper bag filled with the sandwiches.

The sun was shining brightly. Birds were chirping, and all was right with the world.

"I have two weeks off before Internal Affairs decides what to do with me," Johnny said. "What about you?"

"I'm right back to work," Ping said. "Places to go; people to see. Chinese to smuggle into America. You know the drill."

"You can't even get a weekend off?" Johnny said.

"Maybe," Ping said. "But no more than a couple of days."

"We could go to Atlantic City for the weekend," Johnny said. "I have friends who can comp us there."

"You forget. I own a travel agency," Ping said. "I can get my own comps, and mine are legit."

"We don't need separate rooms, do we?" Johnny said.

"Let me think about that," Ping said, smiling. "I might even want separate hotels."

Johnny stopped walking, and he stared across the street.

Paulie, dressed in his best mob suit, stood with his arms folded in a tenement entrance; acting like a bodyguard.

Vito stood opposite Paulie; his arm around a gorgeous young Chinese girl's shoulder.

As was the mob custom, Paulie and Vito took turns whispering into each other's ear.

The gorgeous young Chinese girl, a bored look on her face, read a Chinese-American dictionary.

Paulie spotted Johnny staring at him from across the street. He yelled to Johnny, "Dinner at Mom's tonight?"

Johnny stared at Paulie for a second. Then, with his thumb and forefinger, Johnny made a shooting motion at Paulie.

Paulie feigned horror, and he grabbed his chest; like he'd been shot.

Johnny smiled, and then he turned away from Paulie.

Johnny continued strolling down the street; arm-in-arm with Ping.

"That's your brother? Isn't it?" Ping said.

"Like they say, you can pick your friends, but you can't pick your relatives," Johnny said.

He put his arm around Ping's shoulder and said, "Now, what about you and the FBI? Are you getting a new assignment?"

"No. The FBI is keeping me in Chinatown," Ping said. "The Chinese gangs are still a problem."

"Good. That means we'll be seeing a lot more of each other," Johnny said.

Ping smiled and said, "We'll see about that."

Johnny and Ping stopped walking. Johnny turned to Ping and held her in his arms. Looking into her eyes, he said, "Agent O'Reilly.

I think this is going to be the beginning of a beautiful friendship."

"Oh stop!" Ping said. "This isn't Casablanca, and you're not Humphrey Bogart."

Johnny, mimicking Bogart's voice, said, "Okay sweetheart. We'll cut right to the chase."

He held Ping close, and they kissed passionately.

Suddenly, a dark sedan screeched to a halt in the middle of Bayard Street.

Ah Kay's girlfriend, Lois, jumped out of the car, and she sprinted to where Johnny and Ping were standing.

Johnny and Ping turned towards Lois.

Lois aimed a Glock, and she fired several shots at Ping.

Ping absorbed the bullets in her stomach and chest, and she slumped to the pavement; still in Johnny's arms.

Lois sprinted back to her car. She slid inside and got behind the wheel.

Lois's car careened down Bayard street toward the Manhattan Bridge.

As hordes of Chinese people ducked for cover, Johnny stood and pulled his gun out of his shoulder holster. He fired several shots at Lois's car, blowing out her back window.

Johnny dashed down Bayard after Lois's car; repeatedly firing his gun.

Lois's car sped to the corner. She made a wild left turn; barely missing cars going north and south at the intersection of Bayard and the Bowery.

Then, her car disappeared around the corner.

Johnny put his gun back into his shoulder holster, and he dashed back to where Ping was lying in a pool of blood. He knelt and saw that Ping's unseeing eyes were wide open.

Johnny held Ping's hand, and with tears flowing down both cheeks, he said, "No, God! No!"

Paulie and Vito ran across the street and knelt next to Johnny. Seeing Ping, Vito said, "She's gone, kid."

Johnny stood and said, "I'm going to hunt down that Chinese bitch and slice her to pieces."

A crowd of onlookers assembled and formed a circle around Ping's body.

Paulie scanned the crowd and said, "Easy, Johnny. We'll take care of this ourselves in due time. You can bet your life on that."

Johnny stood and sobbed on Paulie's shoulder. Then, he said, "I loved her, Paulie."

Paulie said, "I know, Johnny. I know."

Siren blaring, an ambulance screeched to a halt in the middle of Bayard Street. Two paramedics pushed through the crowd, and they rushed toward Ping's body.

The paramedics bent down to administer to Ping, and realizing it was useless, they bowed their heads in respect."

Johnny said to his Uncle Vito, "She didn't deserve this."

"Forget it, kid," Vito said. "Things like this happen around here. It's fucking Chinatown. But this won't go unpunished. You have my word on that. My solemn word."

Paulie put his arm around Johnny's shoulder, and he led Johnny away from Ping's body. Vito followed close behind.

Suddenly, Vito turned towards the crowd. His mouth twisted into a snarl and tears fell down both cheeks.

He said to the crowd, "Go home! This show is over! Get the fuck home! I'll take care of this!"

The crowd quickly dispersed in all directions.

Vito turned and paced quickly towards Johnny and Paulie, who were walking slowly with their backs to him.

The three men staggered west on Bayard Street towards Mulberry Street two blocks to the west.

Vito said to no one in particular, "This war has just started. Fuck the cops and fuck the FBI. The streets of Chinatown will be soaked with Chinese blood. And it will be done by my hand and my hand alone."

Sneak Preview!!

Revenge on Mulberry Street
By Joe Bruno

Knickerbocker Publishing Company

© 2018

"Revenge is a dish that tastes best when it is served cold," Don Corleone, from the book "The Godfather."

Chapter One
Johnny Russo - 1984

A stiff wind played havoc with Johnny Russo's wavy black hair as he jogged around Columbus Park, opposite the New York City jail ominously called The Tombs. A muscular 210 pounds chiseled on a six-foot-two-inch frame Johnny resembled an Italian Hercules consumed by his daily labors. Five miles of road work every day is no day at the beach, but if you want to become heavyweight champion of the world sacrifices have to be made.

The scorching noon sun caused pools of sweat to run down Johnny's Christian Dior sweat-suit and straight down into his Puma joggers. Johnny usually started his roadwork at dawn, but last night Benny Bastone, the dispatcher at Prestige Limo, had conned Johnny into taking a late-night ride.

What a hassle that broad turned out to be. Johnny couldn't wait to get his hands around Benny's scrawny neck.

"Johnny, you've got to see this hot broad!" Benny had told Johnny over the two-way radio, mounted under the dashboard of his black stretch Cadillac limo. "Mario drove her two nights ago, and he's been raving ever since. Mario's got a face like a gorilla. But with your good looks, Johnny, you're a cinch to get laid."

Benny knew well what Johnny's Achille's heel was: good-looking broads with long sexy legs and cleavages down to their belly buttons. But, Johnny was madly in love with the drop-dead-beautiful Linda McKay, and there was no way he would risk losing Linda by fooling around with another woman.

Johnny finished his seventh lap around Columbus Park. Eight laps equaled five miles; his daily objective. Johnny missed the soothing feel of his solid gold boxing glove, mounted on an 18-carat gold rope chain, which usually swayed gently around his neck. He had lost both the glove and chain the previous night. Johnny hoped it had merely been dislodged and had fallen onto the floor of his limo. He made a mental note to search for it later.

Johnny sped up his pace. One more lap to go and the last one was pure torture. The booze he had consumed the previous night was taking its toll, and Johnny swore it would never happen again. From now on Johnny would concentrate on two things only: Linda, and his boxing career, in exactly that order.

Johnny's sole mission in life was to make tons of money in boxing, marry Linda and move out of his Little Italy neighborhood, where sinful temptations stood around every corner. He decided to propose to Linda that very night. He couldn't wait to see her lovely face light up like the Christmas tree at Rockefeller Center.

Johnny stumbled through the last few paces of his five-mile jaunt. Then, he made a beeline for the Sons of Italy Social Club located at 91 Mulberry Street, just below Canal Street. The club was located on the ground floor of a red tenement, directly below Johnny's second-floor apartment. Once inside, Johnny collapsed on a weather-beaten armchair, and he picked up an early edition of the *New York Post*.

The club was deserted, except for Chickens, a bookie who ran the club for Johnny's uncle, Carlo Russo. Johnny didn't gamble often, and when he did it was a measly five-time bet: $27.50 to win $25. The local bookies bought Cadillacs with the ten percent vig tagged onto every bet. But the Yankees were in town, and they were on a ten-game winning streak, so Johnny decided to double his usual bet on the home team.

"Hey, Nappy, what's the line on the Yankees?" Johnny said.

"Hey, Dunski, what does it say in the papers?" Chickens said.

"It says the Yankees are favored 9-11."

"Then, what's the fuckin' question?"

Chickens poured himself a glass of water from the sordid sink behind the bar that had more rust on it than an abandoned tugboat. He popped two black pills into his mouth and chugged them down with the warm swill.

Chickens stood straight up, and his head barely cleared the top of the bar.

"Fucking doctors!" Chickens said. "You go visit them in their office, and they rob your fuckin' eyes out. Dr. DiPasquale changed me twenty bucks just to write out a damn prescription. You know what it says on the bottle? 'To be refilled 0 times.' When I run out of these heart pills, I have to go back to that thievin' bastard, so he can write me another damn prescription. That's another 20 bucks down the drain."

Johnny looked up from the newspaper and smiled.

"My heart bleeds for you," Johnny said. "Now, give me the Yankees 10 times."

"Yankees ten times," Chickens said. He put his hand out, palms up. "55 clams. Cash on the barrelhead."

"I'm in my freaking sweatpants," Johnny said. "I'll bring the money down when I leave for the gym."

Nappy Chickens. "Then, I'll write the bet down in my mind when you deliver the cash,"

Johnny let out a deep sigh.

"You're relentless," he said.

Johnny picked up the newspaper and turned it around to the front page.

The headline read: **MAFIA INFORMER TO TAKE THE STAND TODAY!**

Under the headline, a picture of two men, handcuffed to two plain-clothes police officers, extended to the bottom of the page. Both men covered their faces with their free arm and elbow.

Johnny turned to page three. The accompanying story read:

Mafia stool pigeon Gregory Piazza will take the stand today in the trial of Paul Mirada and Tony Palumbo; two reputed Mafia henchmen. It is anticipated that Piazza will tell the jury how Miranda and Palumbo extorted thousands of dollars from him as protection money for his uptown nightclub. Piazza is expected to weave a gory tale of murder and the sale of drugs, most notably cocaine.

The district attorney will also unveil a surprise witness, revealed today to the defense attorneys under the law of discovery, who will corroborate Piazza's allegations. The presence of the mysterious witness will deliver a crushing blow to Miranda's and Palumbo's defenses. According to District Attorney William O'Neil, if convicted, the loss of these two vicious enforcers will greatly diminish the influence of organized crime in New York City."

Johnny threw down the paper in disgust.

"What bullshit!" Johnny said to Chickens. "Did you read this crap on page three?"

"Nah, I never read the back of the paper," Chickens said.

"When the cops make a pinch, there's always a rat involved," Johnny said. "And the stupid public thinks that the police are like Sherlock Holmes, walking around with a magnifying glass inspecting the sidewalk for clues. When, in fact, most cops couldn't find their asses with both hands. Some rat spills his guts, and the cops look like geniuses."

"Who gives a fuck?" Chickens said. "As long as it ain't me getting pinched."

Johnny pushed himself off the armchair, exited the club, and tramped up the steps to his apartment. A cold shower cleared the cobwebs from the night before, and as he shaved, Johnny noticed three long red scratch marks on his neck.

Friggin' Hamilton broad.

Johnny decided he'd tell Linda he got the scratches from sparring.

Johnny donned his black chauffer's jacket, folded his tie, placed it in his inside jacket pocket, and he exited the apartment.

The black limo sat by a hydrant near the corner of Mulberry and Hester, in front of Casa de Carlo, the most exclusive restaurant in Little Italy. Johnny's uncle Carlo Russo owned that place, too. It seemed to Johnny that Uncle Carlo owned everything and everybody in Little Italy.

Unfortunately, a parking ticket adorned the limo's windshield wiper.

Screw Benny, Johnny thought.

If it weren't for Benny's con-job the night before, Johnny would have been back early enough to park the limo in the company garage before it closed.

Johnny ripped the ticket into little pieces and flung them in the gutter. He then checked inside the back of the limo looking for his gold chain and the gold boxing glove.

No luck.

Then, he searched the floor in the front of the limo.

Still no luck.

Johnny slid his hand into the crevice behind the driver's seat. Still nothing.

Shit. A thousand bucks down the fucking drain.

Prestige Limo stood the corner of Houston Street and Sixth Avenue. Outside the garage, five shiny black stretch limos were lined up, double parked, and two black men waxed them like their lives depended upon it. Since Prestige Limo was a mobbed-up business, murder was possible and sometimes inevitable.

Johnny parked his limo behind the last double-parked limo, and he strode into the garage.

Behind a gray stretch limo, a glass window divided the entire width of the garage in half. To the right of the window, a door led to the inner office. Benny did all his business behind the glass window. No drivers were allowed in Benny's office except for Johnny. Benny banished all the other drivers to a cubby-hole inside the garage, which had room for four drivers stuffed in like sardines.

No heat.

No bathroom.

No respect.

Johnny walked past the driver's room and banged on the interior door. A new secretary opened the door. Johnny didn't know her name.

"Where's Benny?" Johnny said as he pushed inside.

The girl noted Johnny's black suit, and he shoved a hand into his chest.

"I'm sorry, but Benny told me no drivers are allowed inside his office," she said.

"I'm an exception," Johnny said. "I'm also his doctor, and he's going to need a doctor after I break his scrawny neck."

Johnny pushed past the startled secretary just as Benny emerged from his private bathroom. When Benny spotted Johnny, his face stiffened.

"Come into the back room," Benny said.

Benny Bastone was an angelic-looking 25-year-old with fine chiseled feature not unlike Felix Unger of television's *Odd Couple*. Benny was born to money and the prospects of an eternally happy life; that is unless one of his drivers ended it for him at an early age. Still, Johnny was Benny's best friend, and maybe his only friend. The other drivers hated Benny with a passion, but they wouldn't dare raise a finger because Johnny was Benny's protector.

Benny led Johnny into his father Mike Bastone's office. A copy of the latest edition of the *New York Post* was lying on his desk. Benny handed Johnny the newspaper.

"I guess you haven't seen this yet," Benny said.

In place of the front-page photo, Johnny had seen earlier, stood one of a dead body covered by a blood-stained sheet. A snapshot of the murder victim sat in a corner inset.

The headline read: **KEY MAFIA WITNESS SLAIN. WAS DUE TO TESTIFY TODAY**.

The color drained out of Johnny's face when he recognized the person in the snapshot.

It was Diane Hamilton.

The story on page three now read:

The body of Diane Hamilton, a reputed drug dealer, was found by an early-morning jogger in an alley near Cherry Street under the Manhattan side of the Manhattan Bridge. She had been shot three times in the back of the head in an apparent mob rubout. Police confirmed reports that there was a considerable amount of money in Miss Hamilton's purse, and robbery was ruled out as a motive.

Miss Hamilton was slated to testify as a surprise witness in the trial of alleged mob enforcers Tony Palumbo and Paul Miranda. Informant Gregory Piazza was schedulable to take the stand today and identify Miss Hamilton as his corroborating witness in this sensational extortion and murder case. Police believe someone silenced Miss Hamilton in order to prevent her from testifying.

Sweat formed on Johnny's brow as he continued reading.

Police have one piece of concrete evidence concerning the identity of the possible killer or killers. A gold boxing glove connected to a gold rope chain was held tightly in the dead woman's hand. The chain is being examined at police laboratories for fingerprints. Detectives are questioning city jewelers and the inhabitants of the city's boxing gyms as to whom the owner might be. Police Commissioner Barry Walden predicted an arrest within the next 24 hours.

Johnny looked at Benny through frightened eyes.

"Benny, you've got to believe me. I didn't have anything to do with this," Johnny said.

Benny shook his head.

"It's not what I believe," he said. "It's what the cops believe. You have an uncanny knack for getting into big trouble, my friend."

Johnny crumpled the newspaper and flung it onto the floor.

"You got that right," Johnny said. "Trouble is my middle name."

Chapter Two

Mary Italiano 1950

Mary Italiano, the youngest of 11 children, was born in 1925 in a tiny two-bedroom apartment at 104 A Bayard Street in New York City's Little Italy. In the early part of the 20th Century, her parents had emigrated to the United States from the province of Salerno, in the Campagna region of Italy, 25 miles from Naples.

Her father, John Italiano, hard-pressed to support his 11 offspring, sold vegetables from a stand in an open-air market on Mulberry Street between Hester and Grand Streets. His wife Carmella took in laundry to make ends meet. As each of the children married and raised their own families, Giuseppe Italiano's financial burden gradually decreased.

104 A Bayard Street is a four-story red brick tenement located between Mulberry and Baxter Streets across the street from Columbus Park. Each floor contains two apartments; one facing the Bayard Street, and the other facing the backyard. By 1930, all eight apartments in 104 A Bayard Street were occupied by John and Carmela Italiano and their married children. Mary, along with her unmarried brother, Joseph, lived with her parents in the front apartment on the second floor.

Directly across the street from 104 A Bayard Street stood Columbus Park's landmark Park House, an open-air dance hall built in 1897 under the administration of William L. Strong, Mayor of New York City.

"I remember my parents going across the street to the Park House every Friday night to dance," Mary told her sister-in-law Rita, who was married to her brother, Johnny. "It was the only night they ever spent alone together. My father sold vegetables, seven days a week, from seven in the morning to ten at night. But on Friday nights he came home at six. All nine daughters had to leave the kitchen so that my father could take his weekly bath in the tub, which was part of the kitchen sink. When he finished bathing, he called all his children into the kitchen and gave them each a quarter. It was the only time I ever saw my father smile."

In the backyard of 104 A Bayard Street stood 104 B Bayard Street, one of the rare back-buildings in New York City. Until the mid-1930s, the toilets for both buildings sat in the backyard of 104 A Bayard Street, or if you wish, the front yard of 1904 B Bayard Street.

"When I was a little girl, I remember my mother taking me downstairs to go to the bathroom," Mary told Rita. "There were only six bathroom stalls for the 16 apartments, so sometimes you had to wait a long time to go to the bathroom. But when I was about six years old a miracle happened: bathrooms, connected by pipes to the kitchen sink, were built in all the apartments. People celebrated for days, but will 11 children in my family, there was still a long wait to go to the bathroom."

Mary's life almost ended at the age of fifteen. While she babysat for his sister Anna's three children, Piero, then six, managed to open the living room window and wander onto the fire escape.

Little Theresa, then five, ran into the kitchen and screamed, "Come quick, Aunt Mary. Pietro's on the fire escape, and he can't get back inside."

Mary hurried into the living room and eased her way onto the fire escape. She grabbed Pietro as he was about to fall and flung him inside the apartment. But she lost her balance and fell over the railing towards the pavement below.

The bright red canopy of the Red Horse Saloon broke Mary's fall. But the canopy collapsed under her weight, and she landed on the head of Jimmy Clark, just as Clark was leaving the Red Horse Saloon after his customary three nightly beers. Miraculously, Mary escaped with only a few bruises. However, Jimmy Clark's neck was broken, and he never walked again.

Whenever Mary saw Samantha Clark pushing her husband's wheelchair, she was overcome by an enormous wave of guilt. Samantha Clark never said an angry word to Mary, but her cold blue eyes said everything.

The Clarks had only one son, Billy. The neighborhood

pranksters called Bill the "pigeon," not because he was an easy mark, which he was, but because he was born with a deformed spinal column that forced him to walk with his head permanently pointed towards the pavement.

The neighborhood jokesters yelled "coo, coo, coo" when Billy Clark waddled down the block. This induced Samantha Clark to carry a huge wooden umbrella, rain or shine, when she accompanied her son on their jaunts. She had honed the point of the umbrella to a sharp point, and if any of the local rabble insulted Billy in his mother's presence, Samantha would shove the point of her umbrella into crevices of their bodies where the sun never shined.

Tall and shapely, Mary Italiano was, without a doubt, the prettiest of the nine Italiano daughters, most of whom were built like linebackers. Mary had raven black hair and penetrating brown eyes. Despite her wondrous appearance, Mary never seriously dated until her early twenties. This was partly because Mary was her eight sisters' "designated babysitter," and partly because her older brothers, Johnny and Joe, were talented professional prizefighters who could do serious damage with their fists. The two bruisers made it clear to the local male rabble that Mary was off limits, or else. That is unless marriage was in the cards, and then the two brothers would adjudicate those proposals on a case-by-case basis.

One bright sunny day in May of 1950, while Mary strolled down Baxter Street, she saw two roughnecks antagonizing poor Billy Clark. Blessed with the same fighting spirit as her brothers, Mary snatched the tops off two garbage cans and chased the two bullies down the block.

After Mary had handled the situation, Billy sat on the stoop of his Baxter Street tenement, put his hands over his face, and cried.

"It's all right Billy," Mary said. She put her arm around his frail shoulders. "Those two have nothing to do except cause trouble. You finished high school, and now you have a fine job at the bank. With your intelligence, you'll do just fine. Those two have trouble even spelling their own names."

Mary and Billy became a regular item in the neighborhood. They were a strange but beautiful sight walking down the pavement arm in arm. Mary so tall, dignified and so beautiful, and Billy with his noble head eternally pointed towards the ground, a proud smile on his face. Thoughtless people shook their heads when Mary and

Billy passed. But Billy's former tormentors kept their distance, and, mindful of the Italiano brothers proficiency with their fists, they minded their manners, too.

Johnny Italiano, now an undefeated heavyweight boxer with great promise, had laid down the law to all concerned: "Make fun of my sister or Billy Clark, and I'll use your heads as a punching bag."

The smart and the not-so-smart all heeded Johnny's warning.

Christmas of 1950 was a sad time for the Italiano family. John Italiano had contracted pneumonia two days after Thanksgiving, and he passed away a week later. His wife Carmella took his passing badly. She screamed at the walls and pulled her hair every night before she finally fell asleep. Her children were uncertain whether to commit their mother to a nursing home so that she could get the proper treatment and not be a danger to herself or to others. But, with Mary being her mother's constant companion, they had universally decided against it.

On Christmas Eve, Mary and Billy attended Midnight Mass together at Transfiguration Church on Mott Street. After Mass, they decided to take a stroll in Columbus Park. Snow felt lightly, but it was not cold, and Columbus Park, with its snow-cover trees, resembled a Norman Rockwell painting.

Billy brushed the snow off a park bench with his handkerchief, and he invited Mary to sit down next to him. The snowflakes melted into the ground as Billy put his arm around Mary's shoulder.

"Mary, I love you very much," Billy said. "I know I'm a cripple, but I also know that looks don't mean everything to you."

"You're a fine-looking man, Billy Clark," Mary said. "Don't talk about yourself that way."

"Thank you, Mary," Billy said, "But I want to make my intentions clear. I have a good job at the bank, and I'm up for a promotion. I know I can provide for you properly, and I'm sure I'd make a fine husband. Mary, will you marry me?"

"Billy, I do care for you very much," Mary said. She wiped a moist spot from Billy's cheek. It could have been a snowflake, but Mary knew it was a tear. "But with the condition my mother is in, I can't make any plans right now. Please forgive me, but now's not the proper time."

Bill stood up, and said, "I understand, Mary. I can understand you not wanting to marry someone like me."

"That's not true, Billy," Mary said. "It's my mother. *I swear it is*. Just give me time. Things will be different when my mother gets better."

Billy offered her his hand, and she took it.

"It's getting late. I'll take you home," Billy said.

Mary stood, and as the bell from Transfiguration chimed, announcing the birth of the Messiah, she tilted Billy's chin upwards and kissed him on the lips. At that instant, she knew that she loved Billy Clark.

"Billy, take me home," Mary said. "I don't remember the last time I felt so happy."

A siren blared, as a police car chased a stolen black Buick down Baxter Street and past the city prison called The Tombs. The driver of the stolen Buick was Bobby Bello who had recently been released from prison after a five-year bit for grand larceny. A stolen car rap would send Bello back to prison for at least another five years, and Bello was determined not to get caught.

The Buick's tires squealed as Bello made a gangster left turn onto Bayard Street.

As Mary and Billy strolled arm and arm on Bayard towards Mary's apartment building, Billy spotted the danger. A split second after he pushed Mary in the back propelling her into the front door of the Red Horse Saloon, the Buick hit Billy squarely, propelling him 30 feet up into the air.

They buried Billy three days later at Calvary Cemetery in Queens. While a pulley lowered Billy's coffin, Mary pushed Jimmy Clark's wheelchair toward the dark hole in the ground. Samantha Clark followed them, propped up under each arm by Johnny and Joe Italiano. As snow fell lightly as it had done three days earlier, Mary threw a red rose onto Billy's coffin.

She bent forward and whispered into Jimmy Clark's ear, "As long as I live, I'll never meet a better man than your son."

Four days later, while Mary attended to her mother Carmella on the second floor, the Italiano family congregated in Anna's fourth-floor apartment to welcome in the New Year. Mary cradled her mother's head in her arms and gently rocked her to sleep. Just before the bells,

Mary trudged upstairs to join her siblings.

Ten minutes after the bells chimed in Transfiguration Church signaling the start of a new year, Carmella Italiano climbed the stairs to the roof. She made the sign of the cross, then jumped off the roof, landing in the backyard between the two buildings.

After her mother's horrible death, Mary Italiano never again ventured into the backyard of 104 A Bayard Street.

Chapter Three

After the holiday tragedies in the winter of 1950, Mary Italiano rarely left the safe confines of 104 A Bayard Street, except to work as a checkout girl, five days a week, from 9 am to 5 pm, at the Lexington Diner on 23rd Street and Lexington Avenue. The only time she ventured out at night was to see her brother Johnny fight at various boxing arenas throughout the five boroughs.

Joe Italiano had retired from boxing after he suffered a detached retina in his right eye, courtesy of a well-aimed and ill-intentioned left thumb delivered by Rocky Kelly at Madison Square Garden. Clancy's mischievous thumb, which was delivered in round two, caused Joe to see two, and sometimes three, Kellys. Despite his handicap, Joe's well-timed left hook, originating from someone where near the ring apron, deposited Clancy into Slumberland in round five.

Joe's eye operation at the Eye and Ear Hospital on 14th Street was deemed a success. But the attending physician told Joe that another thumb could result in complete blindness in that eye. Not wanting to be relegated to selling pencils on street corners, Joe retired from boxing, and instead, became his brother Johnny's manager and trainer.

Mary and her sister-in-law Rita, Johnny's wife, sat ringside at St. Nick's Arena to see Johnny win his twenty-first consecutive fight against King Lewis. An overhand right hand turned the King into a knave at 1:10 of the fifth round.

The punch was so devastating; the referee didn't even bother to count.

During the fight, Mary noticed that between rounds, instead of Joe, a complete stranger was in the ring attending to Johnny as he sat on his stool. Joe stood outside the ring, bent over, whispering instructions into his brother's ear. Still, Mary sensed something was not quite right.

After the fight, Mary and Rita entered Johnny's dressing to congratulate their brother. The newcomer, who Mary later found out to be Dominick Russo, was busy cutting the tape off Johnny's hands with round-tipped surgical scissors. While newspaper reporters fired their questions at Johnny, Joe stood off to the side, seemingly uninvolved in the festivities

"Were you surprised King didn't get up?" one dim-witted reporter asked Johnny.

"Why would I be surprised?" Johnny said, smiling. "A horse wouldn't get up after being hit with that right hand."

While he was being interviewed, Mary thought her brother, with his white shiny piano-key set of teeth, looked more like a Hollywood movie star than he did a prizefighter.

After the interview ended, Johnny called to his wife, "Hey honey-bunny, how about a kiss?" Then, he motioned to Mary. "You too, sis."

Mary gave Johnny a quick buss on the check, and then she motioned for Joe to meet her outside the dressing room door.

Joe complied. And when they were in the hallway, Mary said, "Look, Joe, I don't know much about boxing, but something's wrong. Who's that new guy in Johnny's corner? Why is he doing everything you used to do?"

Joe didn't like being questioned by his younger sister.

He said, "Hey sis, why don't you stick to what you know best, and I'll stick to what I know best," Joe said.

He was not smiling.

"But you and Johnny are barely speaking, even at home," Mary said. "I noticed something has been wrong for weeks. Cue me in. Maybe I can help."

Joe shook his head and said, "Sorry, sis. But this is something I gotta handle myself."

He gave Mary a soft hug and a quick peck on the cheek. Then, he said, "I know you mean well, but don't worry. I have everything under control. Everything will turn out just peachy. Trust me."

Then, he flashed her his biggest smile.

Still, Mary was unconvinced. She knew when her two

brothers were lying. They just weren't very good at it.

Rewind to a few weeks earlier.

His name was Carlo Russo, a rising young hood on Mulberry Street. Carlo had recently been given his button, designating him a "made-man" in a secret society, which had originated in Carlo's town of birth, Palermo, Sicily, in the Thirteenth Century. The American press called this group "The Mafia," but no Mafioso ever used that term. When conversing among made- members, they used the phrase "Cosa Nostra," which, loosely translated meant "Our Thing."

At first, only Sicilians were allowed admission into this esteemed society. But gradually, the rules were loosened. Soon, men whose families came from all part of Italy were invited to join.

Dating back to its time of origin, men who were proposed for membership had to "make their bones" by actually killing someone, or at least be involved in the conspiracy of murder, even it if only meant luring the victim to his death, or cleaning up the blood, or disposing of the body afterward.

But in recent times, the rules had been eased to include men, who were not killers, but, in fact, "good earners," which meant that they put big bucks into their bosses' pockets.

In the Mafia, the money and the prestige flowed up, while the hard work and risk dribbled down.

Once a man becomes "made," or "a wiseguy," he was compelled to follow orders explicitly and without question. If ordered to kill, he must do so in a timely manner, or be killed himself. And if ordered by his boss to a meeting or a "sit-down," he must show up promptly, or be killed, even if he suspected the reason for the meeting was to initiate his own demise.

Carlo Russo was not a good earner. He was a stone-cold killer who actually enjoyed his job. Carlo killed his prey with the same gusto as a Major League Baseball player hitting a grand slam homerun.

Carlo's favorite manner of execution was the icepick, which he would gleefully insert into of his victim's ear, while his free hand covered the dupe's mouth to muffle the screams.

To Carlo, guns were just too damn noisy. But sometimes they

were necessary.

Whereas murder was his profession, boxing was Carlo's obsession. It was the ultimate high for a wiseguy to become the manager of the Heavyweight Champion of the World. It gave him the ultimate respect within the organization and also in the legitimate world.

If the Mafia is about anything; it's about respect.

As an added perk, Carlo knew that if he controlled the Heavyweight Champion of the World, he would have a bearhug on the entire sport of boxing. Then, the big bucks would flow into Carlo's coffers like pressured water from a fireman's hose.

That's where Johnny Italiano came into the picture. Carlo knew that Johnny had the natural ability to beat most of the top heavyweights in the world. And the ones Carlo felt Johnny could not beat, he would make sure that Johnny avoided them like leprosy. Carlo knew that a win over the ageing heavyweight champion Bill Brannigan could be bought at a reasonable price. And if Carlo could not convince Brannigan to be reasonable, then Johnny would fight for the vacant title after Brannigan untimely demise.

The only flaw in Carlo's plan was that he was not, as of yet, Johnny Italiano's manager. But with a little friendly persuasion, and more than a little pressure, Carlo was sure he could convince Joe Italiano to sell him Johnny's contract.

Carlo did not want something for nothing. After all, Carlo was a man of respect. He was willing to pay fair market value for Johnny's contract. And that fair market value would be determined by Carlo Russo and Carlo Russo alone.

That was another perk of being a wiseguy.

Carlo had sat at ringside when Johnny had won his 20th straight fight, a second-round knockout of Killer Keyes. After the fight, Carlo visited Johnny's dressing room with his top aide and enforcer, Butch Salerno.

Carlo, the personification of gangster fashion, was decked out in a $300 black Hickey Freeman shark-skin suit, silk white dress shirt, with a red and white striped tie, and black patent-leather shoes. Barely five-foot-seven-inches tall, but with the strength of a coiled snake, Carlo had a rodent-like face, with a large pointed nose and his upper lip curled down in a permanent snarl.

It was a simple fact that Carlo Russo would win no beauty

contests; which made him all the more determined to gain the proper respect, no matter who, or how many people, he had to kill to do so.

When Carlo entered Johnny's dressing room, Johnny was positioned face-down on the dressing room massage table, while his brother Joe expertly kneaded his brother's bulging back muscles.

"Great fight, kid," Carlo said to Johnny. "You looked fantastic tonight."

Johnny, giving Carlo the Invisible Man treatment, spun around and jumped off the table. Then, he stormed into the bathroom and slammed the door behind him.

Carlo said to Joe, "What's with this kid? He acts like I got bad breath."

Joe wiped his hands on the sides of his pants and extended his right hand to Carlo.

"He's got a bad stomach, that's all," Joe said. "It was nice of you to come to congratulate him. I know he appreciates that, and I do, too."

Joe glanced over Carlo's left shoulder, and he spotted Butch Salerno, like a mastiff, standing guard at the dressing room door. At six-feet-four-inches and as wide as Sicily, Butch's frame blocked the entire entrance.

"I gotta tell you, Joe," Carlo said. "You're doing a great job training your brother. I can tell he's in tremendous shape thanks to you. Most heavyweights today eat themselves out of contention, but not Johnny. He's solid as a rock."

"Well, my brother just loves to train," Joe said. "It's in his blood. He runs seven days a week, rain or shine. The kid's like an animal."

Carlo decided to get right to the point.

"Listen, Joe. Come over to my joint tomorrow night," Carlo said. "I have a proposition I'd like you to consider."

Joe stiffened at the tone of Carlo's voice. Joe knew Carlo was not a man to take no for an answer, especially on his own turf. And those who did say no to him usually wound up wrapped in a rug and thrown into the East River.

"Gee, Carlo, I'm sorry, but I already have plans for tomorrow night," Joe said.

Carlo's eyes turned dark, and he spat out, "Well, break them. Be at my place tomorrow night, eight pm sharp. And no bullshit excuses."

That said, Carlo did an about-face, and after Butch opened the door for him, he stormed out of the dressing room.

Butch started to follow his boss. But suddenly, he spun around and said to Joe, "Remember, eight pm sharp."

While Butch was reinforcing Carlo's edict, Johnny came out of the bathroom

"What was that all about?" he said to his brother.

'Ah, don't worry about it," Joe said. "I got everything under control.

"Why do you treat that asshole Carlo with such respect?" Johnny said. "He's a big load of dog shit."

Joe smiled, and said, "Hey, it costs nothing to be nice. You'll learn that when you grow up and get some manners."

The following night at eight pm sharp, Joe entered the Silver Coin, Carlo Russo's bar and principal place of business, located on Hester Street between Mulberry and Baxter Streets. Joe immediately spotted Carlo, who was sitting at his customary table in the back facing the front door.

Wiseguys never sat with their back to the front door, just in case.

With Carlo was Butch and Carlo's younger brother, Dominick.

Carlo motioned to Joe with a wave of his right forefinger.

"Hey, Joey boy. Sit down and join us for a drink," Carlo said.

As Joe headed towards Carlo's table, Butch shuffled over to the front entrance and locked the door.

It suddenly hit Joe that he was now in Carlo's domain, playing with Carlo's ball, in a game rigged in Carlo's favor.

All things being equal, Joe would rather have been sitting in a sneak pit with his hands tied.

Joe plopped down in the chair Carlo had designated for him, directly across the table from Carlo. Butch and Dominick took seats on either side of Joe, sandwiching him like a red piece of meat between two fat slabs of Italian bread. Joe took note that, besides the bartender, the scar-faced Frankie Fish, they were the only people in the joint.

Things could have been worse, but at this moment, Joe

couldn't think any. But at least he was still alive – if just for the time being.

It was three against one, and any thoughts Joe might have had about fighting his way out had faded away like smoke from a cigarette. Joe knew he could take out any of the three hoods individually with his fists. But the odds of him being victorious against all three at one time was nil, especially since Joe knew all three mobsters traditionally carried deadly weapons.

Carlo took a sip of anisette and washed it down with a gulp of espresso, or "black coffee" as the Italians called it.

"Hey, Frankie!" Carlo yelled across the room to the bartender. "Give Joey here what he wants."

What Joe really wanted was a ticket out of this joint, but when Frankie came over to their table, he ordered a Dewars and club soda instead.

After the bartender returned with Joe's drink, Carlo said, "Listen, Joe, I'll get right to the point. I like your brother's style, and I absolutely love the way you're training him. But what your brother needs is a manager like me who has all the right connections to guide him to the top: the Heavyweight Championship of the World."

Joe sat there dumbfounded, and when he didn't react to Carlo's statement, Butch patted Joe on the back and said in a voice that sounded like gravel, "Drink your drink. You'll feel better."

While Butch patted Joe's back, Joe remembered what an old mob boss had said a generation ago: "The best way to deal with your enemy is to keep patting them on the back until a bullet hole appears between your fingers."

Joe took a sip of his drink, but he still said nothing. There was nothing he could say until he heard Carlo's proposition, and even then, there was not much he could say if he wanted to not leave the joint toes up

When it was obvious Joe was tongue-tied, Carlo resumed his soliloquy.

"Now Joe, I don't want you to get the wrong idea. I don't want you to feel I'm making an unreasonable offer. I want this to be a win-win situation for the both of us. I'm willing to give you ten grand for your brother's contract, and I want that contract extended for a ten-year period. On top of that, I'll give you ten percent of all his future purses. And, as his trainer, I'll also hit you with a cool hundred bucks a week. That's a very generous deal I'm giving you, Joe."

Carlo stood and leaned across the table until Joe could smell the booze on his breath.

"And remember this," Carlo said. "I'm not a man who takes no for an answer. So be smart, and do the right thing here."

Joe removed a handkerchief from his pants pocket and wiped the sweat from his brow. Butch patted his back a second time, and said, "Drink up before your ice melts."

Finally, Joe forced the words out of his mouth.

"Look, Carlo. What you're saying sounds good to me," Joe said. "But you don't know my brother Johnny. He's a funny kid; a real hot-head. If I make this deal without his consent, there's no telling what he might do. He might even retire from boxing rather than have you as his manager."

Carlo's rat-like face twisted into a wicked smile.

"I knew you'd come out with a smart answer like that," Carlo said.

He slowly removed a 38 caliber Smith and Weston revolver from his shoulder holster and placed it on the table.

"I want you to take a good look at this piece," Carlo said. "It's my opinion that a man can accomplish much more with a kind word and a gun, rather than with a kind word alone. You get my drift?"

Butch resumed patting Joe's back. Joe glanced towards Butch, and then towards Dominick. Maybe Joe imagined it, but it seemed to him that Dominick looked slightly embarrassed at what he was witnessing. Joe filed that thought away for future evaluation.

Carlo snatched the gun off the table and slipped it back into his shoulder holster.

"Now, go to your brother," Carlo said. "It's up to you how you present my offer to him. You've always been a smooth talker. I don't care how you do it, but convince your brother I'm making you an offer you can't refuse. And remember my gun. The next time you see it will be the last time you see anything. Capisce?"

Joe downed the rest of his drink in one long gulp. Then, he stood, and said, "Okay, Carlo. I'll speak to my brother right away."

Joe turned and headed for the front door. Butch made like his shadow, patting Joe's back all the way to the front door. Once there,

Butch unlocked the door, and Carlo said, "Joe, I'll give you 24 hours. I want an answer by tomorrow night at 8 pm, sharp."

"No problem, Carlo. I'll see you then," Joe said.

As Joe was exiting the establishment, Butch's right hand spun Joe around, and he said, "Remember. Tomorrow night. 8 pm. Sharp."

Joe shot Butch a sickly smile. Then, he exited the Silver Coin and stepped onto Hester Street.

As he trudged down the block, Joe knew what he had to do. Carlo Russo had given him no choice.

Chapter 4

After leaving the Silver Coin, Joe made a beeline for Tony's Drugstore, located on the southwest corner of Mulberry and Canal Streets. He sped past the soda fountain and slipped into the phone booth located in the back. He dialed Johnny's home number, and Johnny's wife Rita answered the phone.

"Hey, sweetie pie," Joe said. "Is your husband home?"

"Sure, he's home. Where else would he be at this time of night?" Rita said. "And what's with this sweetie pie stuff? Are you in trouble again?"

Good old Rita. Joe knew she was sharp as a tack with a mouth to match. There was no fooling her.

Rather than keep playing this game, Joe decided to do an end-run around her.

"Just put my brother on the phone," Joe said.

Before she could reply, Johnny snatched the phone from Rita's hand.

"What's up, big brother?" Johnny said. "We live in the same building, and you have to call me on the phone. Are you too lazy to walk up two flights of freaking stairs?"

"Listen, Johnny, I'm jammed up," Joe said. "I can't talk on the phone. Meet me in Columbus Park. I'll be sitting on the park benches near the Motor Vehicle Building on Worth, Street on the Baxter Street side of the park."

Johnny glanced at his wife who seemed attached to his left elbow. She was not smiling.

Instead, she bit down hard on the forefinger of her right hand. That was a warning gesture all Italians were all too familiar with.

"Okay, I'll be there in half an hour," Johnny said. Then he banged down the receiver.

"What the hell was that all about?" Rita said to Johnny. "Is he betting those three-legged ponies again? Or, did he lose a bundle in a card game?"

"I'll find out when I talk to him," Johnny said.

"I'm telling you one thing," Rita said. "We're not lending him any more money that he never pays back. I'm saving money in my cookie jar for my new winter coat. He ain't touching a dime of that money."

Johnny had given up arguing with Rita years ago. The little spitfire was only 100 pound soaking wet and bulging with brains; unlike Johnny, who had the reputation of being a might slow upstairs. Rita, who was half-Irish on her mother's side, was always locking horns with his brother Joe, who Johnny knew was the toughest guy in the neighborhood.

So, Johnny did what he thought the wisest thing to do – he lied.

"There's no way we're giving Joe any more money," he said. "He's on his own this time."

Rita stuck her right forefinger under her husband's chin.

"What kind of fool do you take me for?" Rita said. "Joe could sweet talk honey from a beehive. But he ain't getting my winter coat!"

"Look, babe, my brother has his weaknesses, but we both know he's a good man," Johnny said. "He gave up his career to manage me. He was so good; he could have fought even with his bad eye. He quit boxing to manage me, and he's doing a bang-up job, ain't he? I'm undefeated, ain't I? So, let's cut him a little slack. I owe him big-time, and so do you."

"Yeah, I owe him a big kick in the ass," Rita said. She turned her back on her husband. "There goes my winter coat."

"Maybe it won't be so bad," Johnny said. "I'll find out in a few minutes."

"Okay, do what you have to do," Rita said. "Tell Joe I love him, too. But if he ever does this again, I'll wring his freakin' neck."

It was late October, and autumn was still in its youth. Scattered red and yellow leaves dotted the tarred surface of Columbus Park, and a brisk wind blew north on Baxter Street until it dissipated around the corner of Worth.

Joe sat in deep thought opposite the children's wading pool, which had long been the alternative to Coney Island for the neighborhood youths.

Joe was in a jackpot, and he knew it. You just don't mess with a man like Carlo Russo and lived to tell about it. Joe was always more level-headed than Johnny, who would not think twice about making the suicidal move by putting his hands on a made-guy like Carlo. It was up to Joe to break the news to Johnny without putting both their lives in jeopardy.

Joe spotted his brother coming across the softball field and headed in his direction.

Showtime was about to start.

Joe arrived at Joe's bench wearing a blue windbreaker over a white turtleneck shirt. A blue New York Yankee had sat slightly tilted on his head. He sat down next to Joe.

"Hey, what's with the Yankee hat?" Joe said. "You know I'm a diehard Giant fan."

"Screw the Giants," Johnny said. "We just kicked your ass in six games in the World Series."

"Yeah, but DiMaggio is on the way out," Joe said. "Word is out that he's retiring. His legs are shot. Plus, that kid Mantle screwed up his knee in game two of the World Series, and who knows if he's any good anyway?"

"He's better than that showboat Willie Mays, who's always running out from under his baseball cap," Johnny said. "Besides, Yankee Stadium is a ten times better place to watch a game instead of that decrepit the Polo Grounds the Giants play in. It's like comparing the Taj Mahal to a shack in the woods."

"Well, that's good, because Yankee Stadium is where we're headed for," Joe said. "If we can get Bill Brannigan into the ring, we'll fill up Yankee Stadium. With all the Italians and Irish in New York City, Madison Square Garden won't be big enough."

"Enough of this baseball bullshit. What the heck am I doing here anyway?" Johnny said. "We just got our new television set, and I could be home snuggling in front of the TV with my wife."

Joe put his arm around Johnny's shoulder and hugged him tightly.

"Kid, I'm in big trouble," Joe said. "And I need your help to keep my head above water."

"How much cash did you blow this time?" Johnny said.

"A lot more than we both have - *combined*," Joe said. "I lost a bundle at the track, and I tried to make it back by doubling up my bets on the Giants to win the World Series. And we both know how that went."

"Who did you bet with?" Johnny said. "And how much are you in the hole?"

"Ten grand worth, and I owe it to Carlo Russo," Joe said. "But Carlo offered me a way out. I took it, or you'd be seeing me in a pine box at Bachigalupo's Funeral Parlor."

Suddenly, it hit Johnny. Joe had sold him out to cover his betting losses.

"Don't tell me you sold out your flesh and blood to that bastard," Johnny said.

"Listen, Carlo covered my ten grand, plus he gave me another ten grand for your contract," Joe said. "That extra ten grand is yours. You and Rita could do a lot with that money. I'll be okay because Carlo is giving me a hundred bucks a week to be your trainer."

Johnny shook his head in dismay.

"I can't believe you did this to me," he said. "You married me to a mobster. Whatever I do now, people will say Carlo fixed everything for me. You know his reputation in boxing. He buys off everybody, even the New York State Boxing Commission. The referees. The judges. Everybody!"

"What else could I do?" Joe said. "We can't fight a guy like Carlo. He's got his button, and he's surrounded by muscle like Butch Salerno. My only other option was to go on the lam. But if I did that, he'd go after you; go after our family."

"Since when did you become a punk?" Johnny said. "You always taught me not to be afraid of anyone. Now, it's my big older brother who's turned yellow."

Joe jumped up and pulled Johnny to his feet. They stood eye to eye, their noses an inch apart.

"I'm no coward, and you know it," Joe said. "Sure, we could have fought them. Me and you against all the wiseguys on Mulberry Street; not to mention their pals all over the five boroughs of New York City. We wouldn't have stood a chance. We'd both be six feet under if they ever found our bodies."

"I'd rather be dead than sell my soul to the Devil," Johnny

said.

"Listen to me," Joe said. "What do we need this aggravation for? Let me sign over your contract to Carlo. But I promise you that I'll make all the decisions. Carlo just wants to be a figurehead. It makes him look like a big shot with his mob buddies."

"What, you haven't signed over my contract yet?" Johnny said. "Then fuck Carlo. Let him go shit in his hat."

"I can't do that," Joe said. "I'm thinking about the safety of our entire family."

Johnny pushed his brother away.

"Then, you're a friggin' coward like I said," Johnny said.

Joe smacked Johnny hard across the face. Johnny started to fire an overhand right, but he stopped the punch in mid-air.

Suddenly, the two brothers fell into an embrace, and they both spilt tears on the other's shoulder.

It was Joe who spoke first.

"Listen, kid. Let's do it my way, at least for the time being," he said. "Let's give Carlo his piece of paper, and when the time is right, we'll tell him to wipe his ass with it."

Johnny pushed Joe away.

"All right. Do what you gotta do," he said. "But I'll never forgive you for this. For our family's sake, I'll put on a good face. But you'll know how I really feel. My big brother turned out to be a pussy. Who would have fuckin' believed it?"

Johnny spun around and headed across the softball field towards 104 Bayard Street.

The crisp autumn air cut through Joe like a knife. He sat back down on the bench like he was in a deep trance. It seemed like days to him, but it was only minutes later when Joe trudged out of Columbus Park and headed up a steep hill called Park Street to Transfiguration Church located on the corner of Mott Street.

Joe pushed open the massive oak front door and crept inside the church. He was alone, except for three old Italian women with black shawls covering their heads, who stood by the altar up front, lighting candles and mumbling prayers in Italian.

Joe dipped his hand in the holy water and made the sign of the cross. He knelt in the back pew and said a silent prayer.

"Dear God, forgive me," Joe said. "But if it's the last thing I ever do, let me be the one who drops Carlo Russo into the fires of hell."

Chapter Five

It was nine am Thanksgiving morning, and Johnny, after finishing his early morning roadwork, returned to his apartment at 104 Bayard Street with a large white box in his hand with lettering that read: "LaBella Ferrara's Pastry Shop."

He was greeted by his wife Rita, who snapped at him, saying, "What are you freakin' nuts? That's a two-pound box of pastries. If I have to sleep on the couch because we can't have sex while you're training for a fight, you better not even think about eating those pastries."

"Today's Thanksgiving. Forget my diet," Johnny said. He patted his rock-hard stomach. "I'm going to eat like a horse today. I hope you and Mary made enough food. Turkey. Stuffing. Sweet potatoes. And all the trimmings."

Rita smiled, and said, "Okay, if you're going to eat like a horse today, we're going to screw like rabbits this morning."

"It's a deal," Johnny said. "Now, where's my coffee, to go along with these wonderful pastries?"

Rita smiled, and then winked at her husband, "I'll prepare your coffee, but we're going into the bedroom first."

A little after noon, Johnny and Rita bounded down two flights of stairs from their fourth-floor apartment to Joe and Mary's apartment on the second floor. Of course, the two women were preparing the traditional turkey dinner that Americans had expected to consume on Thanksgiving Day. But the turkey dinner would be the final course of an all-day feast and would be the only concession to American customs.

Starting the previous night, Mary had cooked a scrumptious

meat lasagna, while Rita had arranged a tray of Italian antipasto cold cuts, consisting of prosciutto, sopressata, and capicola, as well as Italians cheeses including provolone, asiago, and pecorino. The tray was then decorated with roasted peppers and black and green Italian olives, and rimmed with anchovies.

On the stove, a large cast-iron pot was boiling a dozen artichokes, while the traditional red Italian meat-sauce (or gravy as it is called in New York City) was simmering in a huge stainless-steel pot containing meatballs and Italian sausages. Two pounds of spaghetti was lying on the kitchen table waiting to be cooked after the artichokes were done, and two pounds of homemade cavatelli stood in line to be prepared after the spaghetti.

For starters, Mary placed a tray of cooked chestnuts on the kitchen table next to the antipasto, and the two men began chowing down while the two women handled the cooking on the kitchen stove.

Joe stuffed a piece of cheese in his mouth and yelled to his sister Mary, "Don't forget to keep stirring that gravy. And turn down the heat to low, or you'll burn it."

Mary turned towards Joe with her hands on her hips.

"How about you cook, and I eat?" she said.

Joe belched and inserted another piece of cheese into his yap.

"No, I'm sure you're doing just fine," he said. "But as your older brother, I need to do a little supervision here."

Rita strolled over to the kitchen window and opened it halfway. After the cooking smoke escaped outside, the kitchen inhaled the crisp November air.

"Good, now we can at least breathe," Rita said. "These two mooks ain't gonna lift a finger all day."

Mary poured two glasses of wine from the gallon jug sitting on a side table, and she handed one to Rita.

"Let's get into the holiday spirit," Mary said to Rita.

The women took sips of their wine and then resumed cooking.

"Hey, what about us?" Johnny said. "You didn't pour me and Joe any wine."

"What are you crippled?" Rita said. "Help yourself, and don't break our balls while we're cooking for you two cafones."

It was around three pm when Johnny and Joe fled to the living room to rest up before the main course of turkey and all the Thanksgiving trimmings, which was scheduled for 4 pm. Both were sipping red wine, and on Joe's 17-inch RCA television set the traditional Thanksgiving football game between the Green Bay Packers and the Detroit Lions was in the middle of the third quarter. The Lions, an habitual powerhouse, was kicking the crap out of the lowly Packers by three touchdowns.

Johnny took a sip of wine, and then he said to Joe, "What's up with Carlo's brother, Dominick? He don't know shit from shinola about boxing, and he looks like my chief second between rounds."

"So what?" Joe said. "I'm still giving you all the instructions between rounds from behind you, outside the ring."

"That's no good," Johnny said. "In my next fight, I want you in the ring between rounds, not Dominick. It's easier for me to concentrate on what you're saying when you are in front of me, not behind me. This is my career we're talking about. Let's cut the bullshit. I don't want any screw-ups."

Joe positioned his glass of wine in front of his face and gazed into it like it was a crystal ball.

Finally, he said, "Nah, let's keep it how it is for a while. It makes Carlo look like a bigshot by having his brother in the ring between rounds. Besides, Dom ain't such a bad guy. He's nothing like Carlo. He actually has a good heart."

"It's bad enough Carlo is now my manager," Johnny said. "I don't want it to appear like I'm taking boxing instructions from his jerkoff brother between rounds."

"Look at it this way, kid," Joe said. "The main thing is to keep Carlo off our backs. With Dom hanging around and looking important, Carlo stays away. Get my drift?"

"Yeah, you got a point, Joe," Johnny said. "But I'm still not comfortable with the situation. But I will say one thing. I kinda like Dom myself. Last week he loaned me his car to drive Rita to her mother's house in Brooklyn. I didn't even ask him for the car. I just mentioned I was walking Rita to the subway, and he handed me the keys to his car."

"I told you Dom has a good heart."

"He even stuffed a five-dollar bill in my pocket for gas. He wouldn't take no for an answer."

Joe lowered his voice and leaned towards Johnny. He said in almost a whisper, "I think I know why Dom is being so nice to us. He's stuck on our sister Mary. He even approached me last week about setting up a date between the two of them. I didn't give him a definite answer. What do you think?"

"I think you're freaking nuts, that's what I think," Johnny yelled.

Just then, Rita stuck her head into the room, and said, "Are you two morons fighting again? It's a freakin' holiday. Can't you two keep peace in the family even for one day?"

"We're not fighting," Joe said. "We're just talking loud. We're Italian, for Pete's sake. What did you expect?"

"All right," Rita said. "But just keep it down to a low roar. You're giving me a headache."

After Rita left the room, Johnny leaned forward and whispered into Joe's ear.

"Are you friggin' nuts," he said. "We can't let our beautiful sister go out with that ape. Dom's so ugly when he was born the doctor spanked his mother."

"Come on, your exaggerating. Dom ain't ugly," Joe said. "He ain't Tyrone Power either, but he's a decent looking guy. Besides, Mary ain't doing herself any good by staying home all the time. She needs to get a life of her own."

"But Dom is almost a head shorter than Mary," Johnny said. "When they'd walk the street together, he'd look like her pet monkey. All she'll need is an organ grinders organ and a tin cup."

Joe tried to stifle a giggle.

"Think of it this way," Joe said. "Mary's 26 years old, and the only real boyfriend she ever had was Billy Clark. She's the best-looking of all our sisters, and she's the only one not married. She's always babysitting for one of our nieces or nephews, and she never goes out except to see you fight."

"But he's Carlo Russo's brother," Johnny said. "He has bad genes."

"No, Johnny. Dom is a gentleman," Joe said. "He even suggested that you and Rita chaperone him and Mary on their first date."

"Now, I know you're losing your mind," Johnny said. "That chaperone shit is something they used to do in the old country; not in

America."

"But Mary has nothing to lose," Joe said. "She could dump Dom after one date. Like they say in basketball, no harm, no foul."

"Okay, let's leave it up to Mary," Johnny said. "If she's okay with going on a date with Dom, me and Rita will go along as chaperones. But I guarantee you, Rita will watch Dom like a hawk."

"That's what I'm counting on, little brother," Joe said. "Mary is the apple of my eye. If I thought this was bad for her, I would have told Dom to go fly a kite."

Johnny stood from his chair.

"It's almost 4 pm. Let's go inside and attack that turkey," Johnny said.

Joe glanced at his wristwatch.

"It's not even 3:30," he said. "The turkey's probably not even ready yet."

"Then, we'll pick on what *is* ready," Johnny said. "Like I said, I'm freakin' starvin'."

"But don't discuss anything about Dom until we finish eating," Joe said. "I don't want to kill anyone's appetite, especially mine."

At the kitchen table, Johnny Italiano washed down the last morsel of his Thanksgiving dinner with his sixth glass of wine.

"That's it for me," Johnny said. "if I eat one more bite, I might puke."

As Mary and Rita cleared the table, Joe sat back in the kitchen chair and held his stomach with both hands.

"That's it for me, too," he said. "You two girls really did a great job cooking for us today."

Joe stood up and walked over to where Mary was cleaning the dishes. He hugged her and said, "Hey, Mary, you haven't been getting out much lately, have you?"

"Not really," Mary said. "Why do you ask?"

"I don't know. You get up in the morning, go to work, and then come home and stare at the four walls. I think it's time for you to start thinking about a life of your own."

Mary stared at the ceiling in frustration.

"What do you want me to do," she said. "Hang out in bars

looking for men? You know I'm not like that."

Sensing a commotion, Johnny stood from the table. He grabbed Rita's arm.

"Come on. Let's go into the living room and watch TV," Johnny said.

After Johnny and Rita exited the kitchen, Joe said, "Mary, there's a neighborhood guy who's dying to go out with you. He's an honorable guy, and he did the right thing by asking me to make the introductions. He's very concerned that things are done properly."

"What's his name?" Mary said.

"Dominick Russo."

Mary flashed angry eyes.

"You're kidding me," she said. "Carlo Russo is tearing you and Johnny apart, and now you want to fix me up with his brother? Am I part of that deal, too?"

"Sis, it's nothing like that. Dom's a really nice person. He's nothing like Carlo. He's no John Derek in looks, but I think you and him will make a great match."

"If he's Carlo's brother, how can he be a nice guy?

"Dom's nothing like his brother. He even asked that Johnny and Rita accompany you on your first date. Johnny said it's fine by him."

"What about Rita?"

Joe nodded towards the living room.

"I think that's what they're discussing right now," he said.

Suddenly, Rita booming voice came in loud and clear from the living room.

She screamed, "ARE YOU FREAKIN' CRAZY?"

Mary said to Joe, "I think we better go inside before Rita sticks a fork in her husband's eye."

Chapter Six

At seven am, the day after Thanksgiving, Joe Italiano banged his
ringing alarm clock quiet. The heat from the lone gas heater in the
living room barely crept into Joe's bedroom. So, Joe pulled the
covers over his head and shivered.

Joe knew his brother Johnny now slept warmly with his wife
Rita snuggling next to him, and he decided that, after he married
Mary off to a suitable fellow, he'd find himself a nice, plump, Italian
wife, preferably from the old country.

His ideal wife had dark hair and brown eyes, with a
voluptuous body. She had to be a good cook and not someone whom
you might run into at a Mensa meeting. What Joe didn't need was an
intelligent and bossy ball-breaking wife.

Joe jumped out of bed, and he passed Mary's bedroom. The
door was half open, and Joe noticed that Mary was still sleeping.

"Hey, Mary. Wake up," Joe said. "Don't you have to be at
work at nine?"

His loud voice rebounded off the walls and thudded into
Mary's ears. She pulled the covers over her head to stifle the
commotion.

"Come on, sleepy-head," Joe said. "You heard me. It's time
to get up. We ain't so rich that you don't have to work."

Mary stuck her head from out under the covers, and said,
"Leave me alone. Today's my day off."

"Sorry, kid," Joe said. "Go back to sleep. I'm going out for a
walk to get the newspapers."

"Come back in about two weeks," Mary said.

"Don't get rambunctious. I'm walking all the way down to
the South Ferry where the air is fresh, the coffee is hot, and the
seagulls are more friendly than certain relatives of mine."

Joe gently closed Mary's bedroom door.

In the kitchen, Joe, his frigid breath visible in the cold

apartment, doused his face with cold water to clear the cobwebs caused by too many glasses of Thanksgiving wine. After he brushed his teeth and ran a Gillette razor across this face, he tipped-towed past Mary's bedroom and into his own. He scanned the inside of his closet, and he decided on the Navy pea coat, Navy issued sweater, and a dark blue pair of dungarees – all purchased at the used Army-Navy store downtown on Whitehall Street.

Fully dressed, and with the apartment temperature barely above freezing, he went into the kitchen and turned on all four jets on the gas range to provide more heat.

Joe turned on the kitchen radio, and he heard Frank Sinatra singing "Nancy With the Laughing Face."

Joe thought, maybe I'll give Nancy a call today. He hadn't spoken to his former girlfriend since they had broken up three months earlier.

Nancy Romano was the prettiest girl in Little Italy, but she possessed the temper of the wildest hurricane. She was the daughter of Pete Romano, the benevolent Mafia boss of Little Italy. Carlo Russo, for all his bluster, was merely an underling who took orders from Pete. If Pete Romano told Carlo to sit, Carlo wouldn't even look for a chair.

Pete Romano earned a nice living controlling the neighborhood gambling and loansharking. But Pete strictly prohibited the sale of narcotics. Anyone, who was foolish enough to disobey Pete's non-drug decree, would not be long for this world.

Near the end of the summer, Pete Romano had sent word to Joe to meet him at his Hester Street social club, the hub of Pete's operations, which had a strict "members only" policy. When Joe arrived, he spotted Pete sitting at a circular table where all the sit-downs took place. After Joe took a seat opposite him, Pete folded his hands over his ample gut, and he got right to the point.

"Joe, you've always been a good kid," Pete said. "I've known you since you were in diapers. But it's time that you explained to me your intentions with my daughter Nancy. Nancy will be twenty-five in January, and you must be close to thirty."

"Twenty-nine to be exact," Joe said. "I'll be thirty in December."

"So, what's the story, Joe?" Pete said. "Do you have any plans to marry my Nancy?"

As if on cue, Nancy Romano marched through the front door.

Tall and erect, Nancy looked like a high-priced fashion model. Her jet-black hair was parted on the right side, and it was curled up at both ends, barely touching her shoulders. Her raven eyes had a strange way of flashing when she was angry, that was both attractive and a little bit frightening; especially since she was Pete Romano's daughter.

Nancy wore a black and white polka-dot dress that ended just under her knee, exposing long, shapely legs. She sat next to her father and kissed him on the cheek. Then, she peered coldly into Joe's eyes.

Joe felt nailed to his seat.

Pete Romano turned to his daughter.

"Nancy, I just asked Joe a very important question," he said. "And I'm waiting for his answer."

Nancy leaned forward and continued staring into Joe's eyes like she had x-ray vision into his innermost thoughts. Joe felt her eyes burning through to the back of his skull.

"Joe, we've discussed this before, and you never gave me a straight answer," Nancy said. She tapped the fingers of her right hand on the table like she was playing the piano. "I want to know where we stand, and I want to know now!"

Joe chose her words carefully. Incurring the wrath of Pete Romano was bad enough, but the thought of an angry Nancy Romano sent chills down Joe's spine. Joe figured if he pulled this off and walked out of the club unscathed, he was a better actor than Lawrence Olivier.

He said, "Yes, Nancy, I love you, and nothing would please me more than you someday being my wife."

Joe took a deep breath, and continued, saying "But now is just not the right time. I still have my younger sister Mary at home, and I have my obligations to her. When I marry her off, thing's will be different. Also, I'm very involved in my brother Johnny's boxing career. So, maybe is a year or so I'll be in a better position to contemplate marriage."

Peter Romano started to speak, but Nancy silenced him with an angry wave of her hand.

"WHAT A CROCK OF CRAP!" she screamed. "How about that exotic dancer you've been seeing uptown!"

Joe squirmed in his seat as Nancy continued her tirade.

"Oh, you didn't think I knew about her, did you! The one with the long legs and a gap between them as wide as the Holland Tunnel! Explain her to me, Mr. Italiano!"

For Joe, this was not good news. He decided to take the path of least resistance. He lied.

"What dancer? I'm not seeing any dancer," he said while scratching his head "Oh, wait a minute. You don't mean Lauren McGee, do you? Her brother Bobby's a fighter. He wanted me to train him, but I told him I didn't have the time. His sister asked me to meet her for a drink. She tried to get to reconsider about Bobby, but I……"

What Nancy did next, Joe had seen John Wayne do in Westerns. She jumped to her feet, picked up her end of the table, and flipped it over onto Joe's lap. Bottles and glasses flew in all direction and shattered on the floor.

"YOU THINK I'M A MORON, DON'T YOU!" she screamed.

Both Pete Romano and Joe sat transfixed in their chairs; their mouths wide open, and a shocked look on their faces. Beer dripped onto Joe's lap, but he was too terrified to move.

Nancy screamed louder, "GET OUT OF MY LIFE, JOE ITALIANO! I DON'T EVER WANT TO SEE YOU AGAIN!"

That said, Nancy rushed out of Peter Romano's social club, slamming the door behind her.

Pete stood up and handed Joe a handkerchief. Joe tried to wipe the beer off his pants, but it still dripped down onto his socks, saturating them.

Pete picked up the table and placed it right-side-up.

"Well, I guess that's that," Pete said. "When Nancy gets her balls in an uproar, even I can't control her. I wish you would have thought of a better excuse than that bullshit story about that dancer."

"Sorry, Pete but that dancer was a one-night stand," Joe said. "I don't know how Nancy found out."

"Look, Joe. You and Nancy ain't married yet, and men have to be men," Pete said. "I know how it is. Now, if you had been married, or even engaged, you'd be in deep shit now."

"I know Pete. I know," Joe said.

"Look, kid. She cares for you," Pete said. "Leave her alone

for a while. Give her a chance to cool down. Then, make your pitch, but make it a good one. You hear what I'm saying?"

Joe told Pete that he indeed understood what he needed to do.

Now, it was the day after Thanksgiving, three months after the incident in Pete Romano's club, but Joe still didn't have the courage to dial Nancy's phone number.

"Nancy with the laughing face…"

Sinatra finished the song that Joe was listening to on the kitchen radio.

Then, Joe heard the 7:30 am news.

Hank Kelly, the manager of heavyweight champion Bill Brannigan, was found shot to death in his midtown apartment.

Joe turned up the volume on the radio.

Kelly was found sitting at his kitchen table, face down, with two bullet holes in his forehead. According to the police report, there was no sign of forced entry. The police believe that Kelly knew his killer, or killers, and was engaged in a meeting when he was murdered. The police found three used glasses and a bottle of Irish Whiskey on the table. The police lab dusted for fingerprints, but the glasses had been wiped clean.

Joe poured himself a cup of hot coffee, black, no sugar. His mind raced, listing possible suspects. The radio report continued:

Police say that at this time there are no clues as to who the murderer or murderers may be. But they are investigating Kelly's ties to the boxing world and underworld figures for clues as to a possible motive."

Joe snapped off the radio.

Joe figured Kelly's murder smelled of Carlo Russo. Joe knew for a fact that Carlo had talked with boxing promoters about a possible title fight for Johnny against Bill Brannigan.

But why kill Kelly? Kelly would have jumped at the chance to match the champion with an untested, unknown commodity like Johnny. Brannigan was a wily veteran who knew every trick in the book; legal and otherwise. He would be a prohibitive favorite over Johnny, who had a load of natural talent but was not ready, physically or mentally, to fight a fighter of Brannigan's caliber.

Hank Kelly had always insisted, that for any title fight concerning Brannigan, they would get a significant percentage of the gate, in addition to a guaranteed minimum. With the Irish coming in droves to root for Brannigan, and the Italians doing the same for Johnny, they could fill any park, including Yellowstone Park, and Kelly stood to make a bundle when the fight took place.

Johnny donned his pea coat, pulled navy-blue stocking hat over his ears, and exited the apartment.

Twenty minutes later, Joe arrived at a 24-hour coffee shop/diner at the base of the South Ferry. This small eatery was one of the few 24-hour restaurants in downtown Manhattan, and everyone in Little Italy showed up there sooner, or later, especially after an all-night bender. After picking up a copy of the *Daily News* and the *Daily Mirror*, Joe ordered a hot cup of coffee to stay, and six jelly donuts and six apple turnovers to go.

While Joe sipped his coffee and waited for the counterman to fill his order, he spotted a familiar figure exiting the South Ferry with his back to Joe so that he couldn't see his face. The man wore a black fedora pulled down over his mug, and a grey overcoat buttoned to the top with the collar rolled up over his ears. It was cold at the South Ferry, but not that cold. It was obvious to Joe this man didn't want to be recognized.

The mysterious man made a right turn onto South Street, where he hailed a cab. Joe caught a quick glance at the man's face as he stepped into the cab.

He looked like Dominick Russo.

But why would Dominick Russo be exiting the Staten Island Ferry at eight am in the morning the day after Thanksgiving? Joe wrestled with that question all the way back to 104 Bayard Street.

Chapter Seven

After Joe arrived with the donuts and the morning newspaper, Mary placed a freshly brewed pot of coffee on the kitchen table. Then, he greeted her big brother with a kiss on the cheek.

"Sorry I jumped all over you this morning," Mary said. "I had a terrible nightmare last night, and I woke up all bent out of shape. Funny thing, I can't even remember what the nightmare was about, only that I was scared."

"That's alright, Kiddo," Joe said. "We all have our bad moments." Joe took a sip of his coffee. "Give Rita a call. Tell her and Johnny to come down and sample these delicious donuts I bought by the South Ferry. That's Johnny's favorite place."

"Good idea," Mary said.

She walked into the living room, picked up the phone and dialed Rita's number.

While Mary was talking to Rita on the phone in the living room, Joe flipped through the pages of the *New York Daily Mirror*. There was no mention of Hank Kelly's murder in the news section of the paper. So, Joe flipped the paper over to the sports section in the back. He scanned through a couple of pages and stopped when he saw Dan Parker's boxing column.

While he was reading, Mary came back into the kitchen.

"Hey, Mary. Look what Dan Parker wrote about Johnny," Joe said. "He said Johnny is the best prospect in the heavyweight division. I'm going to clip this and put it in Johnny's scrapbook."

"That's nice," Mary said. "You're going to need a bigger scrapbook pretty soon. By the way, Rita said thanks, but she's staying in bed for a while. I'll save her a few donuts for later on."

"What about Johnny?" Joe said. "Is he still home or did he go out jogging. He better put in an extra mile or two after what he ate yesterday."

Mary smiled. "No, Johnny's still home. That's why Rita is still staying in bed."

"That figures," Joe said. "What the hell? Let them have fun until Monday morning. Then we'll go back to work. I can't let the kid get out of shape. You never know when we might get a big fight."

Joe took a large bite of a jelly donut, and the jelly squirted down onto his chin. After giving his mug a quick wipe, he said to Mary, "What do you have planned for your big day off?"

"I have a three-day weekend to be exact," Mary said. "Me and Rita are going to the movies. There a new Joan Crawford movie playing at the Venice Theater. Everybody is raving about it. We both adore Joan Crawford. She really knows how to handle men."

"Joan Crawford depresses me," Joe said. "Why don't you go see a nice Betty Hutton movie instead. They're always fun. Men like women who are sweet, soft, and cuddly. Not a vampire like Joan Crawford."

"Yeah, guys like you want women you can step all over," Mary said. "By the way, what's the story with you and Nancy Romano? I haven't seen her around lately."

"Ah, we broke up a while back," Joe said. "I had a sit-down with her old man last summer. She wanted to get engaged right away. I told Pete I wanted to wait awhile, and she exposed like a Cherry Bomb. I haven't seen her since."

"See, that's your problem," Mary said. "You always want to be the boss. But with Nancy, you can't be the boss. She has a mind of her own, and you can't take it. You don't want to admit it, but she the perfect girl for you. Men like you need a woman who can keep them in line."

"Better I should marry a cop," Joe said. "If I get even a little bit out of line with Nancy, I have to deal with her father and his gorillas. My life expectancy would be zero, zip, zilch."

"Why don't you just give her a call?" Mary said. "It can't hurt, and you've been close since you were kids."

"I'll think about it," Joe said. "But first, I'm going to have myself another one of these delicious jelly donuts."

At precisely high noon, Joe entered the Silver Coin. He sat at the bar and ordered an espresso. Both Carlo Russo and his brother Dom were conspicuous by their absence; as was Butch Salerno. That was odd, but Joe figured he knew why.

"Is Carlo or his brother Dom around?" Joe asked Frankie Fish the bartender.

Frankie was counting out the new day's cash register bank, and he didn't even look up when he said, "Haven't seen either one yet."

Joe knew asking too many questions in a joint like this was not the wisest thing to do, so he just sipped his espresso and pondered his future.

Since he had retired from boxing, Joe had shaped-up three nights a week at the mob-controlled Fulton Fish Market on South Street, loading and unloading crates of fish. The pay was good; fifty bucks per 12-hour shift. But sturdy young men like Joe swiftly grew old and decrepit schlepping fish on South Street.

During the steaming summers, the workers barely survived the heat; mainly because they slipped in and out of the refrigerated fish lockers. But when the temperature dipped below freezing, it was pure torture. The frigid and damp air blasted through the worker's bones like hot flames through a dry forest. The combination of the unbearable weather conditions and the heavy lifting stamped deep lines on the worker's foreheads and injected arthritis into their bones.

Joe's burning ambition was to save his hard-earned money and move to a warmer climate far from the harshness of the Fulton Fish Market, not to mention the treacherousness of the New York City Mafia.

Joe ordered another espresso and waited. The heavy caffeine from the Italian coffee pumped up Joe's awareness, and he was wide-eyed alert when Carlo Russo trudged through the front door at 12:30 pm.

Carlo sauntered past Joe like Joe was a cockroach on the floor. And after he sat at his customary table, he grumbled to Frankie Fish, who was waiting for his assignment with baited breath, "Espresso with Anisette on the side, and make it quick."

Joe stood up and paced to Carlo's table. He sat in the chair opposite Carlo, and said, "Don't you say hello anymore?"

As soon as Joe saw the rage in Carlo's eyes, he knew he had

made a big mistake.

"Who the fuck are you that I have to say hello?" Carlo said. "You're nothing but a piece of shit to me anyway."

Joe wanted to crack the ugly bastard right in the face, but he knew that since Carlo was a made-man such action would be suicidal.

"Look, Carlo, I didn't come here to argue you," Joe said. "I wanted to talk to your brother Dominick about my sister Mary. What time do you expect him?"

Carlo lifted the glass of Sambuca to his lips and downed it in a single gulp.

"Dom's home sleeping," Carlo said. "We were out playing cards all night. I haven't the slightest fuckin' idea when he'll be around. Now, go pedal your shit someplace else. Nobody invited you to sit in the first place."

Joe knew Carlo was lying. He was sure it was Dom he had seen at the South Ferry.

"Okay, sorry for the intrusion," Joe said. "Just tell Dom that Mary agreed to a date with him tomorrow night at eight pm. He can pick her up at our apartment at 104 Bayard."

"Are you trying to make a fool out of me?" Carlo said. "I'm no messenger boy. Tell him yourself."

Joe's blood was beginning to boil, and before he lost his temper, and probably his life, he said, "Suit yourself. I'll be back later."

Joe walked back to the bar and picked up his change, leaving Frankie a dollar tip.

"Frankie, when Dom comes in, tell him I was here looking for him," Joe said. "Tell him I'll be back around five pm."

Frankie scooped up the buck and said, "Ok, will do."

A split second after Joe exited the Silver Coin, Carlo hurled his glass against the front door, and slivers of glass sprayed in all directions.

Frankie Fish dove behind the bar, expecting to hear bullets. He didn't get back up until Carlo had stormed outside, slamming the door behind him."

After exiting the Silver Coin, Joe hiked to Canal Street where he hailed a cab. He told the driver to take him to Stillman's Gym located at 48th Street and Eighth Avenue, just down the street from Madison Square Garden. While the cabby weaved his way through Midtown traffic, Joe sorted out the puzzle of Hank Kelly's murder. And no matter which way Joe arranged the pieces, it still came up the handiwork of Carlo Russo.

The question was why.

Thirty minutes later, Joe entered Stillman's Gym, and the sweet stench of sweating bodies hit him like a swift kick in the face. No matter his many times Joe slipped into any one of the scores of New York City boxing gyms, dotted throughout the five boroughs, this odor still repulsed him. Some things you never get used to.

Pee Wee, a dwarfish, bald-headed man in his early 70s, ran Stillman's Gym. Before Joe got five feet inside, Pee Wee stopped him with a hand to his chest.

"Hey, fork over the month's dues for your brother's locker," Pee Wee said.

"See Carlo Russo," Joe said. "He's my brother's manager, and he's responsible for the financial side of things."

"No, you see him," Pee Wee said. "He never comes here anyway."

"Okay, Pee Wee. But what did you do with the money?" Joe said.

"What money?" Pee Wee said. "I never got the money. That's why I'm asking you for it."

"No, not that money," Joe said. "I'm talking about the money your mother gave you for charm school."

"Fuck you in spades," Pee Wee said. "Now fork over the cash."

Joe smiled, and then he palmed Pee Wee's bald head like it was a basketball. Pee Wee wiggled and squirmed, but Joe still held firm.

"Hey, let go of my head!" Pee Wee yelled.

"I'll let go if you tell me if Bill Brannigan has shown up yet," Joe said.

"Yeah, he upstairs," Pee Wee said. He pulled a penknife from his pocket, and said, "Now let go, or I'll stab you in the balls."

Joe let go of Pee Wee's head. Then, glaring at the knife, he said, smiling "Who are you scaring with that? It's the size of a toothpick."

Pee Wee was quick with the penknife, but Joe was quicker. Two quick sidesteps and Joe was out of the little man's reach.

Laughing so hard his sides hurt, Joe sprinted towards the steps leading to the second floor. He bounded up the steps two at the time.

For five bucks a month, the fighters training at Stillman's had the privilege of storing their boxing equipment in broken down lockers and showering in an unsanitary cubby hole equipped with one rusted shower head. But befitting his status as the Heavyweight Champion of the World, Bill Brannigan received the red carpet treatment. He had his own private room and his own private shower, that was only slightly more sanitary that one used by the rabble.

Joe stopped at a faded green door. The named "Brannigan" was chicken-scrawled on it in black paint. Joe turned the doorknob, but the door was locked from the inside. Joe knocked hard, three times. But, but no one answered

"Come on, Bill. I know you're in there," Joe said. "I only need a couple of minutes."

A feeble voice said from inside, "I ain't talking to no reporters."

"Hey, Bill. It's Joe Italiano. Johnny's brother."

In seconds, the door opened and Bill Brannigan, all six-feet-four-inches and 230 pounds of him, blocked the entrance.

"What's on your mind, Joe?" Brannigan said. His voice had an edge to it.

"Bill, I just want to tell you I'm sorry about Hank Kelly," Joe said. "I also wanted you to know I had nothing to do with it, and I was shocked when I read it in the papers this morning."

Brannigan turned and lumbered inside. He did not close the door, and Joe followed him in. Brannigan sat hunched on a wooden bench, and Joe sat next to him.

"Yeah, you're sorry, alight," Brannigan said. "Hank was just another cockroach, and you guys stepped on him."

"No, Bill, you have it all wrong," Joe said. "Carlo is my brother's manager on paper, but I call all the shots. At least that's the agreement we have. But as soon as I read about Hank, I knew Carlo was involved. I just didn't know why. Was Carlo trying to broker a fight between you and Johnny? If he did so, it was without my knowledge or consent."

Brannigan stood and shuffled over to his locker. He removed a pint of Irish whiskey from the top shelf and took a long gulp. Then, he sat back down next to Joe and offered Joe the pint bottle. Joe grabbed it and took a small sip. It burned all the way down. He handed the bottle back to Brannigan, who finished it off.

"Yeah, Joe, I guess you're on the level," Brannigan said. "You've always had the reputation of being a stand-up guy. I couldn't believe it when I heard you and your brother were mixed up with that scumbag Carlo Russo."

"Yeah, Bill. I couldn't believe it either. It wasn't my doing, but that's another story. Tell me what you know, and I swear it won't leave this room."

"Funny, I was just sitting here wondering what I'll tell the cops when they show up. I was going to lam-it, and let my lawyer issue a statement or something. And I still might do it if I have the time, but it's probably too late. They'll probably be here any minute. So, before the cops get here and I clam up, here's what really happened."

A week ago, Carlo Russo had cornered Brannigan just as he was leaving the Stillman's Gym. Butch Salerno was with Carlo, and after Butch strong-armed Brannigan into an empty tenement hallway, he stuck a 38 caliber pistol into Brannigan's ribs.

"You and your manager Kelly are going to come to my joint on Mulberry Street," Carlo had said. "Tonight at midnight. Don't be late, and don't make me come looking for you."

"Our first mistake was going down into Carlo's territory," Brannigan told Joe. "As soon as we entered his joint, they drew pistols and forced us into the back room, where Carlo, that ugly fuckin' midget, slapped Hank in the face. Once. Twice. Three times. Then, he told Hank that me and Johnny were going to fight for the title within three months, or else. That was no problem with me. Your brother's good, but he's green. It should be an easy fight for me. I'd beat him on experience alone."

Joe figured, with the way Brannigan was hitting the Irish whiskey, experience may not be enough.

He let Brannigan continue.

"But the kicker was that I had to go into the tank. They had a gun to my head. What was I to say or do? So, I agreed with the proposition. Carlo told me he'd give me fifty grand to throw the fight. Twenty-five grand after I signed the contract, and twenty-five grand after I splashed. After we left the joint, Hank told me not to worry. He said he knew how to handle those guinea bastards. That's the last I heard about it until last night."

Brannigan stood and went to his locker. He removed another pint of Irish whiskey, took a swig, and offered the bottle to Joe. Joe refused it with a wave of his hand.

"So, what happened last night?" Joe said.

Brannigan spoke as he paced the room.

"It was after midnight, and I was sleeping," Brannigan said. "The phone rang, and I heard Hank's voice. It sounded like he was crying. The bastards then made me hear Hank beg for his life. He was saying over and over, 'Don't kill me. I have four kids and a sick wife.' And that's the truth. I knew it, but Carlo didn't care. Then, I heard the shots. Two quick ones. And, a second or two later, another shot. Then the phone went dead.

"I prayed that it was all a sick joke; that they were just trying to scare me. But this morning, I heard the news on the radio. That's all I can tell you. I was waiting for Carlo to get in touch with me. When you knocked on my door, I figured you were here as Carlo's boy."

"So, what are you going to do?" Joe said.

"What am I going to do? I tell you what I'm going to do. I'm going to fuck everybody. I'm retiring and giving up the crown. I ain't taking no dive, and I'm going out as champ."

"Think this through, Brannigan," Joe said. "You think Carlo's going to let you retire? Just like that? You have a wife and kids?"

"Yes, me and Millie have three kids, and one is on the way."

"So, that's it," Joe said. "He'll grab your wife, or one of your kids, and hold them for ransom until you do the right thing. You don't know Carlo like I do. He'll do anything to get what he wants, and a human life means nothing to him."

Brannigan sat on the bench, put his head between his hand, and began sobbing. His massive back muscles bobbed up and down.

"But what can we do?" Brannigan said between sobs.

Joe stood up and approached a speed bag hanging from the ceiling in the back of Brannigan's dressing room. He started tapping the bag slowly, first with his left hand; then with his right hand. Then, with both hands, increasing the intensity and the cadence.

Ratta tat tat… Ratta tat tat… Ratta tat tat…………..

Joe stopped attacking the speed bag, and he turned towards Brannigan

"No way, Brannigan. No freakin' way!" Joe said.

Then, he turned and hit the bag with increased speed and vengeance.

"We'll make our stand now," Joe said, while still punching the bag. "If we don't stop Carlo, he'll be up our asses the rest of our lives."

"But how?" Brannigan said. "How do we fight back at Carlo with all the muscle he has surrounding him?"

Joe fired one last right hand at the speed bag that knocked it completely off its moorings, propelling it against the back wall with a *TWARP*!

Joe turned back to Brannigan.

"Don't worry, Bill," Joe said. "I have an ace in the hole that even Carlo can't trump. And now I'm going to use it. In spades."

Chapter Eight

Joe exited Stillman's Gym, and he made a beeline for Gilhooley's Bar, a smelly dive on Eighth Avenue just down the block from Stillman's. Gilhooley's was a joint where hordes of greedy fight managers contrived their next fistic move. The crowd in Gilhooly's resembled rush hour at Port Authority, but instead of bus tickets, flesh was sold at pennies a pound.

The décor at Gilhooley's was early Depression, and the cockroaches outnumbered the customer at a rate of ten to one. The hundred-foot rotten oak bar ran from the front entrance back to the urine-stained men's room, inside of which a sign read: *We aim to please. Your aim will help.*

Gilhooley's owners saw no need, nor did they have any desire, to construct a companion ladies room. No real lady would ever enter Gilhooley's anyway.

Fight managers who frequented Gilhooley's were notorious for treating their fighters like slabs of beef; impersonally pushing them around from fight to fight, with the endgame being the swift upward explosion of the fight manager's bottom line. Bigtime fight managers wore hundred-dollar suits and sparkling pinkie rings. Most fighters were lucky if they had a decent pair of shoes.

Gilhooley's bartender was a pleasant chap named Lefty Porter, who had been an excellent welterweight before the Second World War. An exploding mine in France had left Lefty with a 12-inch stump for a right arm, but despite the handicap, Lefty could fill a drinker's beer mug as well as any of this two-fisted contemporaries.

Joe ordered a draft Schaefer, and Lefty expertly drew the beer from the tap with his right stump, while his left hand held the mug in place.

After Lefty placed the mug in front of Joe, Joe said, "Has

Ray Brown been around lately?"

"Not so much," Lefty said. "He ain't been feeling well these days. He spends most of his time at home. The word is that he's disgusted with the fight racket, and I can't say I blame him."

"Could you contact him for me?" Joe said. "It's really important."

"You're not making a comeback, are you kid?"

"Not me, Lefty. I like the idea of being able to see with both eyes. It's my brother Johnny. He's ready for the big time, and I've taught him all I know. I needed someone like Ray Brown to apply the finishing touches."

"I don't know, kid. The last time I spoke with Ray, the old man was really down on the sport. He said he lost all interest in the game when you quit on him. "

"I didn't quit Ray," Joe said. "The doctors did that for me."

"You know what I mean," Lefty said. "Ray's tired of everybody lying through their teeth. Ray just couldn't deal with them bastards anymore. He's like a square peg trying to fit into a round hole."

Joe downed his beer. He ordered another and Lefty obliged him. Joe took a sip and headed for the single pay phone located at the back of the bar. Pat Petrone, a washed-up pug five years older than Joe, screamed into the phone as Joe respectfully waited in line eight feet behind him. Still, Joe couldn't help but hear Petrone's rampage.

"Please see what you can do for me," Petrone whined into the phone. "I'm in good shape, and I really could use the cash. I'll give you six good rounds, or whatever you need. Then, I'll take an exit. Your boy will look good, and everybody will be happy."

The phone clicked dead on the other end.

"Son of a bitch!" Petrone yelled.

Petrone turned and spotted Joe. He put his head down and hurried past Joe without even saying a word.

Poor bastard, Joe thought. They just don't know when to quit; especially when they're broke, which is most of them.

Joe dropped a dime into the phone and dialed Nancy Romano's phone number.

After three rings, Nancy's answered, "Hello, the Romano residence, who's speaking?"

Joe took a deep breath, and then he said, "Hello, Nancy. It's Joe."

Nancy hesitated for a split second, and then she snapped, "Oh, so it's the great Joe Italiano. What do you want? My father's not home."

"I don't want to speak to your old man," Joe said. "I wanted to speak with you. Could you meet me, say, in an hour?"

"Joe, I thought I made it clear I didn't want to be bothered with you anymore."

Joe felt his heart sink into the pit of his stomach.

"Look, Nancy. This will only take a few minutes," Joe said. "The last few months have been miserable for me without you. Please."

"Okay," Nancy said. "I'll give you exactly ten minutes of my time. Where do you want to meet?"

"How about Dave's Corner?" Joe said.

"All the way down on the corner of Canal and Broadway? That's some hike from Mulberry Street."

"Yes, but we've had some of our best times there; having a burger and a Cherry Lime Ricky. You remember, don't you?"

"Okay, I'll be at Dave's Corner in an hour. But I can only give you a few minutes. I have a date."

"Give me ten minutes, and I guarantee you you'll break that date," Joe said.

"Don't hold your breath," she said.

Then, the phone line went *click*.

Dave's Corner is one of the few luncheonettes in Manhattan that never closes. Because it's one of New York's taxi driver's favorite hangouts, the place is just as crowded at four in the morning as it is at four in the afternoon. Sometimes busier.

Besides the usual inside seating, there is outside counter service on the Broadway side, where a white-capped counterman dispensed such delicacies as egg creams, malted milks, hamburgers, hot dogs, French fries, and an occasional knish: a square potato pancake that is usually cut in half widthwise and slapped with a schmear of mustard.

Joe arrived at Dave's Corner 15 minutes early, and he sat at the first booth by the cash register, facing the front door. It was the only empty booth in the establishment. Almost all the other tables were taken by men Joe knew as cab drivers, engaged in conversations on topics ranging from baseball to boxing, to their favorite pastime - horse racing. Joe had gotten tips on three-legged ponies by the very men sitting at these tables. Partly for that reason, Joe made believe they were strangers.

From the side window, Joe could see the Canal Street entrance. He ordered a Cherry Lime Rickey and waited.

In minutes, a black Cadillac double-parked in front of Dave's Corner. A tall, elegantly dressed man wearing a grey pinstriped suit exited from the driver's side. He sauntered around the front of the car to the passenger side like he was modeling his suit, or, maybe, his walk. He opened the door, and Nancy exited the Caddy. She looked like a fashion model ready to traipse down the runway.

Joe's heart almost stopped.

The man in the suit took her hand and led her to Dave's front door. He opened the door for her, but before she went inside, she threw her arms around the man's neck and kissed him on both cheeks. The man then strode back to his car, sat behind the wheel, and waited.

Joe shook his head. If that man was Nancy's date, Joe had a rough road ahead of him.

As Nancy approached Joe's booth, Joe stood at attention. He tried to kiss her on the lips, but she turned her face and offered her cheek. Joe reluctantly took the offer, and said, "Have a seat."

After she sat opposite him in the booth, Joe said, "Who's the man in the grey suit?"

"That's my boyfriend," Nancy said.

"Nice suit," Joe said. "Nice car, too."

"Look, I'm here like you requested," Nancy said. "Please get to the point."

"How about a Cherry Lime Rickey?" Joe said. "Just like old times."

"No, thank you," Nancy said. "That's ancient history anyway."

Joe decided this was no time for half-measures, so he reached across the table, held Nancy's hands in his and said, "Nancy, I truly love you, and I want you to marry me."

For an instant, Joe wasn't sure if he said what he just said, or maybe he was dreaming. But when he saw the stunned look on Nancy's beautiful face, he knew he was indeed awake.

"Alright, let's cut the crap," Nancy said. "What do you really want?"

"I just said it," Joe said. "Do me the pleasure of being my wife. My life is miserable without you. Please, just say yes."

Nancy shook her head with a curious smile.

"Joe, I know you like the back of my hand," she said. "There must be a catch. What is it? Are you in some kind of trouble."

"I'm always in trouble, you know that," Joe said. "But right now my only problem is that I don't have you. Say yes, and I'll speak to your father tonight; ask him for permission to marry you."

Nancy reached across the table, cupped Joe's face in her hands and kissed him gently on the lips.

"Joe Italiano, you certainly pick the most romantic places to propose to a young lady," she said. "No ring. No champagne. No candlelight. No romantic music. And here we are in Dave's Corner surrounded by cab drivers scratching their butts and picking their noses."

Joe smiled. "You forgot the belching and cursing."

"Yes, that too," Nancy said. "So, how can I refuse? Of course, I'll marry you. It's about time I made you an honest man. The only question is what took you so long? And why now? I know you too well. There's something else you're not telling me."

"Wait, did you just say yes?" Joe said. "What about the man outside waiting in his car?"

"Yes, I said yes," Nancy said. "And don't worry. I'll take care of him."

That said, Nancy rose from the table and went outside. Joe watched as she leaned into the driver-side window and said something to the man. After the man rolled up the window, he started the car, turned left on Broadway and headed south.

Nancy went back inside Dave's Corner and sat in the booth next to Joe.

"Who was that guy and what did you say to him?" Joe said. "I never saw him before."

"Just an associate of my father's," Nancy said. "I was trying to make you jealous. I just told him to go see my father and tell him you wanted to talk to him tonight."

"Did you tell him why?

"Of course not. That's your job to talk to my father. I'm not going to make it any easier for you."

"Wow, that was quick," Joe said, smiling. "You don't leave anything to chance, do you?"

"Of course, it was quick," Nancy said. "Once I have a fish like you on the line, I'm going to reel you in, pronto, before you wiggle away. Now, tell me what you have been neglecting to tell me. Don't forget, I read the newspapers, too. It's Carlo, right? You and Johnny are in trouble, right?"

Joe told Nancy everything; from the time Carlo forced him to sell him Johnny's contract, up until Joe's meeting with Brannigan earlier in the day.

"Joe, you should have come to my father right away when Carlo threatened you about Johnny's contract," Nancy said. "Carlo works for my father. My father has Carlo firmly under his thumb. If you had done that right away, none of this other mess would have ever happened."

"Looking back, you're probably right," Joe said. "But I thought I could handle Carlo. But after what happened to Hank Kelly, I see that I can't handle everything. I just want to make sure nothing happens to Johnny or the rest of my family. As for me, I can handle myself. Carlo's not the only tough guy in Little Italy."

Chapter Nine

Joe and Nancy walked blithely hand and hand north on Mulberry Street. They turned right on Hester Street and stopped in front of Nancy's apartment building, two doors down from her father's social club.

Joe kissed Nancy on the cheek and said, "I'll see you at eight at your father's club. I'll bet he'll be surprised by what I have to say, that's for sure."

Nancy smiled and said, "Not as surprised as I was this afternoon."

She kissed Joe full on the lips, then headed into her apartment building.

Joe's feet barely touched the pavement as he glided down Mulberry Street to the Silver Coin. Once inside, Joe spotted Carlo and Dom sitting in the back at their customary table. Knowing his place, Joe sat at the bar next to two neighborhood men and ordered a draft beer.

After Frankie Fish placed the beer in front of him, Joe said, "Did you give Dom my message?"

"Sure did," Frankie said. "He seemed really excited that you wanted to talk to him."

Joe downed his first beer, and he ordered a second.

He told the bartender, "Frankie, do me a favor. Me and Carlo ain't getting along too well these days. Tell Dom I want to speak with him when he finished talking with his brother."

"Sure thing, Joe," Frankie said.

Five minutes later, Dom bellied up to the bar and sat next to Joe. He offered his hand and said, "What's up, Joe."

Joe shook Dom's hand. He noticed Dom's eyeballs were

streaked in red, and he was wearing the same overcoat he had worn that morning at the Staten Island Ferry.

"Dom, I spoke to my sister Mary, and she agreed to go on a date with you," Joe said.

"That's great," Dom said. "When would it be convenient?"

"How about tomorrow night at eight?" Joe said. "It will be six of us. You and Mary. Johnny and Rita. And me and Nancy."

"I thought you and Nancy were on the outs?" Dom said.

"We were," Joe said. "But now we're back together, for good."

Dom seemed slightly taken back. Then he said, "How about if we eat at Forlini's at 5 Baxter Street? It's a small joint, but the food is great."

"That sounds good," Joe said. He decided to throw a curveball, when he said, "Did you hear what happened to Hank Kelly last night? Someone put a couple of bullet holes in his forehead."

"No. This is the first I'm hearing about it," Dom said.

"I wonder why somebody would want to murder Kelly," Joe said. "He always seemed like a nice guy to me."

Dom stiffened, and said, "Well, I head he don't like us Italians too much. Always throwing around disgusting words like guineas and greaseballs. Maybe the potato-picker got what he deserved."

Dom stood up from the bar, and said, "Well, me and my bother have some unfinished business to take care of. You'll have to excuse me."

The two men shook hands, and Dom said, smiling, "I'll meet you people over at Forlini's tomorrow night at eight sharp. "

That said, Dom headed back to Carlo's table.

Carlo was not happy when Dom returned to his table.

"What was that big conversation all about?" Carlo said.

Dom lowered his eyes in apparent shame, but it was really fear. For as long as he could remember, Dom could never look directly into Carlo's eyes. When he did, he saw the Devil.

"I asked Joe if he could set me up on a date with his sister, Mary," Dom said. "We're on for tomorrow night at Forlini's."

"Mary's a good looking broad," Carlo said. "But if you ask me, the whole family stinks. Especially that scumbag you just spoke to."

"Joe told me something else," Dom said. "But I don't want you to get sore."

"What the fuck? You playing games with me?" Carlo said. "Spill. I want to know what he said."

"Joe said he's back with Nancy Romano," Dom said. "They're coming out with me and Mary tomorrow night. Johnny and his wife Rita, too."

Dom waited for the explosion. He wasn't disappointed.

Carlo stood and banged his fist on the table.

"That fuckin' cunt! I've been asking her out for weeks, and she kept putting me off," Carlo said. "Now I know why. Not that I give a fuck about her to start with. But she's Pete Romano's daughter, and that would have put me in real tight with Pete."

"Look, don't get all sore," Dom said. "Maybe Joe was just blowing smoke. I'll find out tomorrow night."

"Yeah, you do that."

Dom hesitated before he said, "Joe also asked me about Hank Kelly. You don't think he knows anything, do you?"

"Now don't get all spastic on me," Carlo said. "Joe's a smart guy. Too smart. It's been all over the papers. He's probably put two and two together already."

Carlo leaned across the table and stuck his forefinger into Dom's chest.

"Now don't say nothing stupid to him tomorrow night," Carlo said. "You'll do anything for a piece of pussy, you ugly bastard."

"I'm not ugly," Dom said weakly, his head down, like a beaten man.

"Well, you ain't Clark Gable either," Carlo said.

Dom decided to change the conversation.

"That was a good idea of yours; having me ditch the pistol off the Staten Island Ferry," Dom said.

"Yeah, there's probably enough rods in the water between Manhattan and Staten Island to start another World War," Carlo said.

Carlo's face got mean again.

"By the way, are you sure nobody spotted you pitching the

pistol overboard?" Carlo said. "Besides being ugly, you ain't exactly Albert Einstein either."

Dom's face turned a bright red, and his voice cracked when he said, "I'm fuckin' positive no one saw me. I threw the gun into the water from the bottom deck of the ferry. And it was in a paper bag anyway. Besides, you're not so smart yourself. It was my idea to take the stairs when we left Kelly's apartment. If it were up to you, we could have been spotted in the elevator. So get off your high horse!"

"Okay, so you're a fuckin' genius," Carlo said

"Just don't sell me short, I've got brains, too," Dom said.

Carlo smiled when he said, "If brains were gunpowder, you wouldn't have enough to blow your nose."

Carlo was relentless in his insults, so Dom decided to change the subject again.

"Well, what's our next move?" he said.

"Simple," Carlo said. "All we have to do is lay low for a while. Let Brannigan stew in his own juices. Then, we'll pay him a little visit. He'll fold like a cheap suitcase. Those Irish cocksuckers got big mouths, but when you get them alone, they have no balls."

To Carlo, the act of killing was almost like getting laid. Even though Dom was present when it happened, Carlo described his killing Hank Kelly to Dom with savage glee. While Carlo gave his brother a detailed account of Kelly's murder, Dom's stomach began to churn. He couldn't get any sleep all day long. Every time he shut his eyes, trying to nod off, all he could see where Kelly's dead fish eyes staring at him.

"The only thing I regret is not cutting the Irish fuck into little pieces and feeding them to the rats in Chinatown," Carlo said. "Imagine, that rat bastard telling his cop uncle in the Fifth Precinct what we were planning. What did he expect me to do about that? Nothing?"

Late Thanksgiving night, Carlo had told Dom, "You know what? I think we should pay a little visit to Hank Kelly at his apartment."

As soon as Kelly had opened his front door, Carlo stuck a gun in his face and ordered him to sit at the kitchen table. After Carlo cracked Kelly across the face a few times, Kelly quickly admitted that he had told his cousin, Captain Jim Clancy of the Fifth Precinct, all about Carlo's plan for Brannigan to relinquish the heavyweight title under duress.

Finally hearing the truth from Kelly's own mouth, Carlo went berserk. He ordered Kelly to phone Brannigan, and while Kelly spoke to his fighter, Dom had held the muzzle of his gun against Kelly's forehead. But when Carlo ordered Dom to shoot, he just froze. Carlo could kill someone, then devour a roast beef sandwich dripping with blood five minutes later.

Dom was cut from a different cloth.

When it was apparent Dom was not going to shoot Kelly, Carlo screamed, "Give me that fuckin' gun!"

Carlo snatched the gun from Dom's shaking hand, and he fired two bullets into Kelly's forehead, propelling his head backwards and killing him instantly. Then, he fired another one into the ceiling, just for fun.

But Carlo was not finished.

After hanging up the phone, Carlo grabbed Kelly's bloody hair and smashed his head, face-first, onto the glass table top, pulverizing the glass into little pieces.

Since that horrible moment, all Dom could see was Hank Kelly's mangled face dripping blood onto the fractured glass.

Carlo summoned Frankie Fish from behind the bar with a wave of his scrawny forefinger.

"Two more Jack Daniels, straight up," Carlo said.

After Frankie returned with the drinks, Carlo said to Dom, "You coming with me to the trotters in Yonkers tonight? I have a tip on a horse that can't lose. I want to get there before the odds drop."

"No, I'm going home to get some sleep," Dom said. "I'm still bushed from last night."

"Okay, but I want you to remember one thing," Carlo said. "Tomorrow night I don't want you making a fool of yourself with this Italiano dame. You'll be out in public, and everyone knows I'm your brother. Everything you do reflects on me."

"Don't worry, I'll be cool," Dom said. "It's only our first date anyway."

"And another thing," Carlo said. "Be careful with that

asshole Joe Italiano. He's got more moves than a belly dancer."

"Joe ain't such a bad guy," Dom said.

As soon as the words left his mouth, Dom knew he had made a mistake.

"*Joe ain't a bad guy!*" Carlo screamed. "That's because you want to get into his sister's pants! Remember, you're a Russo, and all us Russos got pride. Don't you dare do anything to embarrass the family name."

Dom started to rise from his chair, but Carlo reached across the table and grabbed his arm in a vice-like grip. He screamed loud enough for the bartender to hear, prompting Frankie Fish to decide this might be a good time to go into the men's room, which he did; just in case things got ugly. The two neighborhood men at the bar sat silently, trying to ignore the commotion in the back.

"Reme*mber, watch out for those Italiano brothers!*" Carlo yelled.

Dom stood up and shrugged off Carlo's grip on his arm.

"Don't worry about me. I can take care of myself," Dom said. Then he added, "Besides, I get along fine with the Italiano brothers. You don't because you have a personality conflict. I don't have that problem."

Carlo became so angry at his brother's statement; he struggled to speak. When he couldn't get the words out of his mouth, he backhanded Dom, hard, across the lips, causing blood to trickle down Dom's chin.

Dom started to react in kind, but then he changed his mind.

"*Don't you ever speak to me in the tone of voice again!*" Carlo bellowed. "*I'm your older brother! Don't you ever take a stranger's part over me again!*"

Dom wiped the blood off his chin with a handkerchief. Then, he glanced at the bar, where the two men sat turned around facing them with their mouths open.

"Carlo, you're my older brother, and I respect you," Dom finally said. "But don't you ever put your hands on me in front of people again."

Carlo reached for the gun in the holster under his left armpit, but after spotting the two men sitting at the bar, and Frankie Fish peeking from inside the bathroom, he changed his mind.

Carlo yelled at Dom, *"Now get the fuck out of here! You*

make me fucking sick! You have no fuckin' respect!"

Dom stared at Carlo, hard, for a second. Then, he did an about-face and headed for the exit. But before he got there, Carlo picked up a glass from his table and hurled it at Dom. The glass missed Dom's head by inches and smashed against the wall. Glass flew in all directions.

Dom turned and glared at Carlo. Then, he left the Silver Coin without saying another word.

Carlo looked like a man possessed by the Devil.

He yelled in the direction of the two customers at the bar and Frankie Fish, *"No fucking respect, that's what I get!"*

Then, he pointed his finger at his bartender, and said, "And you. You're getting too friendly with that Joe Italiano. Don't forget who's the boss around here."

As Frankie Fish cringed in fear, Carlo approached the bar.

He yelled at the bartender, "And if I ever find the register short again, I'll cut off all your fingers."

Carlo turned and exited the Silver Coin, slamming the door behind him.

A minute later, the two customers also exited. And as soon as they were outside, Frankie Fish returned the ten-dollar bill he had taken from the register an hour earlier.

Chapter Ten

Joe Italiano entered Pete Romano's Social Club on Hester Street at precisely eight pm. After he stepped inside, he spotted Nancy sitting next to her father at Pete's usual table, her hands sedately folded on her lap. At this time of night, the joint was usually buzzing with activity, but Joe noted that they were the only three people present.

Joe wondered where were the men guzzling beer and playing knock rummy; the neighborhood's favorite card game. And where were the men watching sports on the small black-and-white 17-inch RCA Victor television set mounted high on the wall behind the bar? And most importantly, where were the bookies quickly tallying the day's betting results?

Why was the joint empty?

But before Joe could contemplate that question, Pete motioned for Joe to sit opposite him. When he did, Nancy smiled broadly. And it was Pete who broke the heavy silence.

"Hey, Joe, how about a little wine?" Pete said. "Nancy says you have something to say to me, and I've always said that a little wine loosens up the tongue."

"Now that you mention it, I could use a little glass of wine," Joe said.

Pete poured Joe a hefty portion of red wine into a 12-ounce glass from a gallon jug he had placed on the floor next to his chair. Joe eradicated three-quarters of the wine in one long gulp.

Joe glanced at Pete, who now wore a benevolent smile on his chubby face. Nancy winked at Joe, but Joe was so petrified, he barely noticed. With a lump in his throat, Joe knocked off the rest of his glass of wine

"You see Pete, me and Nancy had a little talk today," Joe said. He glanced at Nancy, then at his empty glass. "Can I have a little more wine?"

"Sure, you can have all the wine you want," Pete said. He handed Joe the entire gallon bottle. "Help yourself."

Joe resisted the urge to lift the jug to his lips and guzzle the wine like a *cafone*. Instead, he shakily poured himself a glass, spilling some of it on his lap.

Joe forced the words out, saying, "Look Pete. We, er… We decided that we… er… er… We thought it would be a good time for us to. Er… that is, er… If you would only give us er… uh… uh…"

Nancy couldn't contain it any longer. She burst out laughing and said, "Go ahead, Daddy. Tell this moron you know already. This poor bastard is scared shitless."

"No, I'm not," Joe said. "I'm just a little nervous. What the heck! Pete, I like your permission to marry my, no, I mean marry *your* daughter."

Pete's grin erupted into a smile the size of Sicily.

"Jesu Christi, he finally spit it out!" Pete said. "I thought the man was going to have a heart attack right here in my club. Then, what would I tell the cops?"

"Go ahead, Daddy, *tell him*!" Nancy said. "Before he *does* drop dead on the floor."

Pete stood reached across the table and offered his hand to Joe.

"Of course, you have my permission to marry my daughter. My only question is 'What took you so long.'"

As if on cue, the club's back door opened, and half of Little Italy scrambled through the door, yelling, ***"Surprise!"***

Johnny, Rita, and Mary led the stampede, and Johnny grabbed Joe in a playful bear hug, almost fracturing Joe's ribs.

"It's about time you broke down and did the right thing," Johnny said.

Rita and Mary took turned hugging and kissing Joe and doing the same to Nancy.

Suddenly, about a dozen hired waiters scurried through the back door carrying folding tables and large trays of hot food. They set up shop, transforming the grubby social club into a fancy catering hall.

After hordes of people surrounded Joe and Nancy offering their congratulations, Joe squeezed Nancy's hand, and said, "Wow, that was some surprise trick you played on me. I didn't have a clue this was going to happen."

"Sorry, Joe, but it was my father's idea," Nancy said. "I couldn't help telling him when I got home. And you know him. He always wants to make a big splash. He had all his men running all over the neighborhood rounding up all the people and rounding up all the food. It was crazy what he accomplished in just a few hours. Look at all these people!"

"He *is* Pete Romano," Joe said. "People jump when he tells them to."

"Even you," Nancy said.

"Especially me," Joe said. "I jump even higher."

From the corner of his eye, Joe spotted Carlo Russo entering the club, alone.

Carlo approached Joe and offered his hand. When Joe took Carlo's hand, it felt like a damp cold fish.

Carlo was truly pissed he had to give up going to the Yonkers Racetrack to attended a party for a man he absolutely loathed. But Pete Romano was the boss of Little Italy, and Carlo was merely one of his men who took his orders, whether he liked them or not.

"Congratulations," Carlo told Joe in a hissing monotone.

Carlo quickly bussed Nancy on the cheek, and then he fled to the bar to get himself come much-needed booze.

Nancy had noticed the visible animosity between the two men, but she decided to say nothing.

The party lasted well into the night. Every few minutes, Pete called for a toast to "my beautiful daughter and my future son-in-law."

And every time Pete called for a toast, everybody drank, which led to the revelers getting loaded, all except Joe. All party long, Joe kept his eyes glued to Carlo, who was drinking heavily at the bar and obviously not having a very good time. Carlo's face displayed a perpetual sneer, which became more sinister the more he drank.

The sight of his Carlo's malicious face kept Joe sober all night.

At around three in the morning, the party began to disintegrate. Johnny and Rita were the last to depart, leaving Nancy, Joe, and Peter Romano the only ones left in the joint.

Pete rubbed his belly as he said, "Well, I guess it's about time for me to call it a night too." He turned to Nancy, and said, "If your mother were still alive, she'd be grabbing me by the ear by now."

Pete handed Joe a set of keys. "Here, Joe. You lock up for me. Okay?"

"Sure thing, Pete," Joe said.

Peter exited the social club through the front door with a gleam in his eye and a stagger in his step.

"We better go home and get some sleep," Joe said. "With all the excitement I forgot to tell you we're going out tomorrow night as chaperones on Mary's first date with Dom Russo at Forlini's. Rita and Johnny are coming along, too. Dom did the right thing and asked me for my permission to date my sister. And it was his idea for all of us to come as chaperones."

Nancy faced dropped when she heard the news.

"You're letting your sister date Carlo's brother?" she said. "Besides, she's a head taller than him!"

"So what? Dom's a good guy," Joe said. "He's nothing like his brother Carlo."

"Yeah, maybe you're right," Nancy said. "Dom seems like a decent guy. But I cringe at the thought of having Carlo in the family."

Nancy gently took Joe's hand and said, "Joe, there's something I have to tell you. Carlo's been hounding me for a date for months, but I kept putting him off. He couldn't even look me in the eye tonight."

"That explains his actions tonight," Joe said. "Carlo doesn't like me to start with, but tonight he was doubly pissed off at me, and now I know why."

Joe and Nancy exited the social club. Joe locked the club door and walked Nancy back to her apartment on Hester Street.

They arrived at her tenement building, and Joe kissed Nancy, first on both cheeks, and then full on the lips.

"That should keep you until tomorrow," Joe said.

"Just barely," Nancy said, and then she turned and entered the building.

On his walk back to 104 Bayard, Joe decided he would soon have to take on Carlo Russo head to head. Even though Carlo was a killer, he didn't frighten Joe.

Joe said to himself, "Fuck Carlo. He doesn't understand that I'm Sicilian, too."

Chapter Eleven

Dom Russo rolled out of bed at eight am on Saturday morning totally exhilarated. Tonight was the night he had dreamed about for so long. He was finally going on a date with the lovely Mary Italiano.

How could a man be so lucky?

The previous night, wanting to look and feel his best for his date with Mary, Dom had slipped into bed at eight pm. There was no usual trip to the track. And no Friday night drinking marathon, the objective of which was to find a gorgeous young girl to take home, but which always ended with Dom going home alone with copies of the *New York Daily News* and *New York Daily Mirror* stuffed under his arm.

Dom had just turned thirty, but he had never had a steady girlfriend. His short, stocky body, combined with a weak-chinned face, had always made Dom less than a popular attraction amongst the local female population.

Dom didn't have much luck with the uptown or Brooklyn girls either.

After tending to his morning necessities, Dom slipped into dark-blue shark-skin trousers, and a grey-and-blue Italian knit shirt. He opened a suit bag and removed a three-quarter-length soft black leather coat, which he donned over the Italian knit. All three had been purchased the evening before at Al Kaplan's on Canal Street.

Dom examined his appearance in a full-length mirror mounted on the back of his bedroom door. Satisfied, he exited his apartment and walked down the four flights of stairs to the Mott Street pavement below.

As he traipsed down the block, Dom sniffed the marvelous rich aroma of the baked bread emanating from Parisi's Bakery, which had been a neighborhood staple since 1903. On an average day. Dom would knock down at least two loaves of Parisi's 25-cent Italian bread, which led to him carrying almost 200 pounds on his five-foot four-inch physique. Dom knew that the scrumptious combination of Italian pastries, pasta, bread, red and white sauces, and garlic-coated delicacies shortened the lifespan of the Italian/American male. But what's the good of being Italian if you can't eat?

Dom made a right on Hester, and he stopped at Gino's Barbershop, owned and operated by an Italian Immigrant who had come to this country three decades earlier with just the clothes on his back and a five-dollar bill in his pocket. Gino employed no other barbers, and sometimes men had to wait more than an hour to sit in Gino's coveted barber chair.

Dom entered the establishment, and he heard the tingling of the doorbell signaling to Gino that a new customer had arrived.

"Good morning, Gino," Dom said. He took off his leather coat and hung it on the wooded coat tree. "I see I'm next."

The shop was empty except for a youngish uniformed police officer on whom Gino was displaying his tonsorial talents.

"Good morning, Dominick," Gino said in his broken English accent. "Captain Clancy just called, and he'll be here in a few minutes. So Clancy is next, and then you are after him. Have a seat. I'll get you some coffee. Black or brown?"

Unlike in most of the rest of the world, in Little Italy black coffee meant espresso, and brown coffee meant the traditional American coffee usually served with milk and sugar.

Dom ordered the black coffee with a little Anisette on the side, and before he could take a sip, Captain Jim Clancy, the commander of the Fifth Precinct on 19 Elizabeth Street, strode through the front door. Clancy's precinct supposedly protected the Lower East Side, which included Little Italy. But in truth, Fifth Precinct cops had very little to do with respect to controlling crime, since the only crime in the Fifth Precinct was organized crime; Italian and Chinese.

Clancy was a giant of a cop, standing six-feet, six inches tall, the maximum height allowed for a New York City police officer. His hair resembled newly-fallen snow, which enhanced Clancy's image as a respected figure of authority.

Clancy hovered over the diminutive Gino. He patted the barber's bald head and said, "Good morning, my little greaseball friend."

Gino stiffened. He ran his forefinger across his pencil-thin moustache, as he said, "Good morning Ill Duce. I see you're always on time for your free haircut."

Clancy removed his navy-blue regulation three-quarter length cloth winter coat resplendent with gold buttons, and he hung it on the coat tree next to Dom's leather coat. Clancy sat in the chair next to Dom and waited. He didn't even slightly acknowledge Dom was in the establishment.

A few minutes later, Gino spread talcum powder onto the young cop's neck. Then, he used a wooden bristled brush to sweep it off with a flourish.

The young cop stood, reached into this pocket, and handed Gino a crisp dollar bill.

"Thank you, young man," Gino said. "I hope you captain is just as generous."

Clancy shot the young cop a dirty look, and then he plopped down in Gino's barber chair.

Gino spread a white pin-striped barber sheet over the good Captain's torso and secured it in the back with a safety pin.

As Gino performed his magic, Clancy peered into the mirror in front of him, and he noticed Dom's face was buried in the *New York Daily News*.

"Hey, Russo," Clancy said. "I heard Pete Romano's daughter got engaged last night to Joe Italiano."

Dom said, without looking up, "I know they're dating, but I don't know nothing about no engagement."

"Yeah, I guess you're so low on the mob totem pole, they don't tell you anything," Clancy said. "By the way, tell your brother Carlo I'm sending over a new man on Monday to collect. His name is Rubenstein. And tell Carlo to make sure the amount is right. I don't want to come to your place myself all pissed off. You know what that means."

Whenever Police Headquarters assigned a new sergeant to the Fifth Precinct, Clancy made him in charge of the weekly graft collections. The new sergeant made his rounds every Monday during the eight am to four pm shift. He arrived at each location carrying a large blue leather satchel, and when he left, the satchel was always substantially heavier. When his rounds were completed, he would deliver the satchel to Lieutenant Morelli at an uptown bar, the location of which changed every week, just in case. Then, the sergeant would immediately vacate the premises.

Lieutenant Morelli took the satchel into the bathroom and into one of the stalls, where he would drop his drawers so as not to be disturbed. After counting the cash, Morelli took out 15% for himself and 10% for the new sergeant. He put the rest of the money back into the satchel, with a slip of paper saying how much money was in the satchel, and then he made a beeline for the Port Authority Bus Terminal where he placed the satchel into a locker, the key to which he would give to Captain Clancy the following morning. Captain Clancy would pick up the satchel as soon as possible, and take it home with him where he would have some privacy.

After taking half the remaining money for himself, Clancy would divide the rest of the money by the number of cops on the take in the Fifth Precinct, which was just about everyone. The resulting amount was the amount of money the new sergeant would dispense Tuesday to the crooked cops, which consisted of most of the Fifth Precinct.

This was the way it had been done in the Fifth Precinct for decades, and everything went smoothly.

No muss. No fuss. No risks involved.

And that suited Captain Clancy just fine.

How else could he have afforded his massive home in Bay Ridge, Brooklyn, containing four bedrooms, four baths, a two-car garage, a fully remodeled basement complete with a bar and pool table, and a heated swimming pool? Of course, Clancy was shrewd enough to put the deed under his wife's mother's name, just in case someone got nosey.

Gino put the finishing touches on Clancy's free haircut: parting his hair, powdering and de-powdering his neck, and patting his back, signally Clancy's haircut was done.

Clancy rose to his full height and examined himself in the mirror. Then, he said to Gino, "Gino, my man, here's your big tip. Bet the five horse in the fifth race at Aqueduct, across the board. That's the biggest tip you'll ever get from me, wop-face."

Gino forced a half-a smile, and said, "You're such a big

sport, Captain. You toss around nickels like fucking manhole covers."

"Fuck off, Dago," Clancy said, as she donned his overcoat.

As Clancy opened the door to leave, Gino yelled at him, "Hey, Captain, you know I had a wet dream last night. I dreamed I slit your throat with my straight razor while I was shaving you. It was the best load I shot in years."

Without answering, Captain Clancy exited Gino's Barbershop and slammed the door behind him.

Dom Russo took Clancy's place in Gino's barber chair.

As Gino was fastening the barber sheet around Dom's neck, Dom said, "I don't know how you take that arrogant donkey's bullshit."

Gino said, "What choice do I have? What choice do we all have? We all paid up before Clancy got here, and we'll all be paying after Clancy is gone. That's just the way it is, was, and always will be."

"Yeah, I guess you're right," Dom said. "But I know one thing for sure, there's going to be a long line to piss on Clancy's grave when he's six feet under."

While Gino cut Dom's hair, Dom closed his eyes and smiled. He thought of nothing but the beautiful Mary Italiano, who he would formally meet for the first time in just a few short hours.

At this very moment, Dom was as happy as he had been in his entire life. And he was intent on not doing anything that could possibly spoil his bliss.

Unfortunately, circumstances beyond his control would occur that would throw his life, and the lives of those he loved, into the chasm of despair.

Chapter Twelve

Captain Clancy paraded double-time from Gino's Barbershop to the Fifth Precinct just a few short blocks away.

The Fifth Precinct, located at 19 Elizabeth Street, was the oldest police precinct in the city. Built in 1881 for less than $40,000, the now-decrepit building, both outside and inside, stands between a row of aging tenements, whose storefronts house mostly Chinese restaurants, whose daily garbage attract hordes of hungry rats. The cat-sized rats make their grand appearance at the early morning closing time, when the restaurant owners pile their trash in front of their establishments, tolling a silent dinner bell for the tens of thousands of the four-legged creatures on the prowl. By the time the Sanitation trucks pick up the rotting garbage a few hours later, more than half of it has already been eaten by the rats.

Clancy marched through the front door, and his spit-shined boots thumped loudly on the wooden floor. He shot a summary salute to the desk sergeant sitting on the right at a decrepit desk located three steps off the floor. The desk sergeant, at least fifty pounds overweight, was chomping down on a huge meatball sandwich he purchased from Tony's Italian Deli just down the block.

The desk sergeant quickly put down the sandwich and said. "Good morning, Captain."

Clancy shook his head in disgust, and said, "Sergeant, every time I see you, you're stuffing your face with a big Italian hero. Haven't you ever heard the word - salad?"

The sergeant wiped the red meat sauce off his lips with a napkin, and then he said, without much conviction, "Yes, sir!"

"Get me the Silver Coin on the phone," Clancy said. "I want to speak to Carlo Russo. Transfer the call to my office."

Clancy marched down a long pea-green corridor, with the paint chipping on both sides, past the detention cells and into his private office. He locked the office door and availed himself of the private bathroom reserved for the ranks of Captain and above.

Once inside, he unzipped his fly, and using his faithful right hand, he induced a huge erection. Seconds before ejaculation, he stuffed his penis back into his pants.

Clancy had learned this neat trick years back when he attended the New York Military Academy in the rural town of Cornwall, 60 miles north of New York City. Of course, this maneuver was not in the official military manual but was taught on the sly by the amply-named Commandant of Cadets, Dick Hertz.

The lesson was depicted thusly: *"If you want to become as mean as a slithering snake before combat, effect, then abort, the completion of the act of masturbation."*

His blood boiling to the pressure point, Clancy went back into his office and picked up the phone. Frankie Fish, the bartender at the Silver Coin, was on the line.

"What the fuck are you on the line for?" Clancy said. "I want to speak to your boss."

Frankie Fish said, "Carlo told me to hold the phone while he went to the john. He'll be right back."

Clancy wondered maybe if Carlo had attended the New York Military Academy, too.

After two minutes had expired, Carlo's voice appeared on the other line.

"Captain Clancy, what a pleasant surprise," Carlo said. "How nice of you to call. What can I do to help you?"

"Cut the bullshit?" Clancy said. "You have some nerve keeping me waiting on the phone."

"Well, you know. Nature calls."

"After you hear what I have to say, I guarantee you nature is going to call you again."

"Just get to the point, Captain. My time is valuable."

"Alright, you Dago fuck, I'll get to the point. You killed Hank Kelly, and I can prove it."

"Is this some kind of joke, Captain?"

"No joke, Carlo. In case you didn't know it, Hank was my eldest sister's son. He was the apple of Lucille's eye. Damn, he was a fucking altar boy until he graduated high school. And just last week Hank told me about a problem he was having with you."

"Listen, Captain, just in case you're taping this conversation, murder is not my line of work. I take a few bets here and there, and that's it. I make a few bucks, and you make a few bucks. In fact, you make a damn good living just on my back alone."

"Yeah, and I'm going to make a lot more."

"Well, meet me at my place so we can speak in private," Carlo said.

"Your place? My ass!" Clancy said. "Do you think I'm some sort of moron. I know what goes on in your place. Meet me in an hour at Patrick's Pub on 32nd Street and Broadway. It's right opposite Gimbals. And make sure you're alone."

That said, Captain Clancy slammed down the phone.

Forty-five minutes later, Butch Salerno's black Buick eased into an illegal parking spot by the hydrant in front of the Broadway entrance of Patrick's Pub.

"I'll see you back in the neighborhood," Carlo said.

Carlo Russo emerged from the passenger's side, and he entered the bar, as Butch directed the Buick south on Broadway.

During the week, Patrick's Pub was pick-up paradise, where on any given night, fifty to a hundred women and men congregated with the hope of finding a sleeping partner for the night. However, on the weekends, when most of the local businesses in the neighborhood were closed, the place was practically deserted.

A solitary sanitation department worker sat at the bar and guzzled down a mug of beer, as the bartender tried to solve the daily *New York Times* crossword puzzle. Two waiters sat at the first table by the door, and when Carlo entered, they quickly threw in their gin rummy hands and stood at attention.

"May I help you, sir?" a tall, blond beach-boy-type waiter said to Carlo.

"Table for two," Carlo said. "The last table in the back will be fine. I'm meeting someone here."

Carlo always made it a point to arrive early for any meeting, just in case of an ambush, which was not entirely out of the realm of possibility considering he was meeting a police captain with an attitude, who had the law on his side, even when he was breaking the law.

Carlo sat at the round table, facing the door. He ordered a gin and tonic and waited, without great patience.

Ten minutes later, Captain Clancy burst through the front door, resplendent in his full dress uniform, metals sparking. He eyed the sanitation worker at the bar, and then he marched back to where Carlo was sitting. He hovered over Carlo like a vulture ready to dive-bomb a rotting carcass.

"Give me your seat," Clancy said. "I'm not sitting with my back to the front door."

Carlo stood up. He gave Clancy his seat, and *he* sat with his back to the door.

Carlo said, "Captain, I think you've been watching too many cops and robbers movies."

Clancy stood up and said, "Stand up again. I have to frisk you."

Carlo stood up, raised his hands over his head, and said, "Now I know you've been watching too many cops and robbers movies. Do you think I'm stupid enough to carry a rod when I'm meeting a fuckin' New York City police captain?"

Clancy gave Carlo his best professional frisk, even fingering between Carlo's legs.

"Okay, you're clean," Clancy said.

Both men sat back down.

"You sure you ain't queer, touching me between the legs like that?" Carlo said.

Clancy grunted, and when the waiter arrived, he ordered a scotch and soda.
They sat in uneasy silence until the drink arrived. When the waiter left, Clancy took control of the situation.

"Okay, Carlo, this is the deal," Clancy said. "I know you killed Hank Kelly, and I have a witness locked up tight. You thought you were smart taking the stairs at Hank's place, but you were spotted and positively identified from mug shots.

"You're full of shit," Carlo said.

"Am I? Are you willing to take that chance?"

"You're still full of shit. Cops like you always lie through their teeth."

"Look, I can go to the District Attorney's office with my story," Clancy said. "But why should I when I can make you pay through the nose?"

"So, that's your angle," Carlo said. "It figures. I never met a cop who didn't have his filthy hands out."

"You shouldn't complain," Clancy said. "I'm going to save your Guinea ass. But only if you come across."

"What's the numbers?"

Clancy smiled and said, "So, I got your attention. This is the deal. I want ten grand up front. That's for my sister Lucille so that she can bury Hank properly."

"Bury him properly?" Carlo said. "Why don't you just stick a torch up his ass and roast some fucking marshmallows?"

"I'll ignore that tasteless remark; you're nothing but a Goddamn animal anyway," Clancy said. "Besides the ten grand, I want $200 a week for as long as we both are breathing. By my estimate, you make about ten times that, so it won't break your back."

Carlo leaned back and folded his arms. "Do have anything else in mind?" he said.

"No, that's it," Clancy said. "Ten grand up front and two hundred clams a week. That's a small price to pay for not spending the rest of your life in jail. Think it over, and get back to me. You have twenty-four hours."

Carlo drained the rest of his gin and tonic, and then he looked straight into Clancy's eyes.

"I've already thought it over, Captain," Carlo said. "Shove your offer, and your supposed witness, up your ass. I ain't biting."

Carlo spotted thick red veins bulging in Clancy's neck.

Clancy started to speak, but all he could manage were short gurgling sounds like he was drowning in his own saliva. Clancy grabbed for his drink, and he downed the scotch and soda in one huge gulp.

"You know, you're a stupid fucking wop!" Clancy said. "Here I am throwing you a lifeline, and you're acting like an idiot. Play it smart, and take the deal. Do the right thing here."

"I am doing the right thing," Carlo said. "I'm telling you plain and simple – *GO FUCK YOURSELF!*"

Carlo reached across the table and poked his forefinger into Clancy's chest. Clancy stiffened like someone had just inserted an iron pole up his butt.

"Listen to me, copper," Carlo said. "I figure you made up the story about the witness. You cops like to bullshit and figure guys like me will lap it up. But I ain't buying. In any event, you're right about one thing; you're not asking for that much money. I can easily afford it. But I'm not going to give you the satisfaction of shaking me down."

Before Clancy could reply, Carlo reached across the table and grabbed Clancy's wrist.

"Listen to this, Captain," Carlo said. He leaned forward and said in almost a whisper, "Sure, I blew out Kelly's brains, and I'll do the same to you if you give me any more trouble. Fuck you. And fuck your badge."

Carlo released Clancy's wrist, and Clancy's mouth started to twitch rapidly like he was going into convulsions.

Clancy stuttered, " Youuuuuu… mother… fuckerrrrrrrrrrr! *I'LL KILL YOU MYSELF!"*

Clancy started to reach for his police issued revolver under his armpit, but Carlo just smiled and Clancy froze.

"You won't do a fuckin' thing, captain," Carlo said. "Not with those four witnesses in the joint. You're not going to do a fucking thing except put your tail between your legs and get the fuck out of this bar. *NOW WALK!* I'll pay the tab. That's the least I can do considering what I did to Hank, that prick nephew of yours."

Clancy lurched to a standing position, he eyes wide open and his mouth agape. Carlo thought the big cop was going to have a heart attack right in front of him.

Instead, Clancy staggered to and out the front door of Patrick's Pub.

Carlo dropped a twenty-dollar bill on the table, and he too exited Patrick's Pub. He got outside just in time to see Captain Clancy flag down a passing police patrol car. Carlo opted for a cab.

"The corner of Baxter and Canal," Carlo told the cabby.

Ten minutes later, Carlo paid the cab driver in front of Most Precious Blood Church on Baxter Street, just north of Canal. He entered the church, dipped his right finger into the holy water, made the sign of the cross, and genuflected. Then, he counted out ten twenty-dollar bills from a huge wad of cash he had in his pocket and deposited them into the poor box. He faced the altar, genuflected a second time, and then he exited the church.

Carlo didn't exactly know why he donated $200 a week to the Catholic Church. He just knew when he did it made him feel a whole lot better than when he first had entered the church.

And if there was indeed a God, which Carlo sincerely doubted, maybe the man upstairs would give Carlo a special dispensation when it came time for Carlo's Judgement Day.

Just maybe.

Captain Clancy ordered the policeman who was driving the squad car to drop him off at the corner of 14th Street and Second Avenue.

"I'll take the subway from here," Clancy said.

As soon as the patrol car disappeared, Clancy hot-footed it to a dilapidated tenement on 12th Street, just east of Second Avenue. After glancing both ways, Clancy slipped into the building. He climbed the stairs and stopped at apartment 3 C. He took off his police hat and rang the bell. A tall, slender young man, barely in his twenties, with straw-colored hair, opened the door. He motioned for Clancy to take a seat on the couch.

"Can I get you a drink?" the young man said.

"Double Johnny Walker Black on the rocks," Clancy said.

The young man went into the kitchen. He returned with the drink, and Clancy downed it in one huge gulp. He handed the glass back to the young man.

"Another," Clancy said.

After the young man filled Clancy's glass a second time, Clancy imbibed it just a little slower than he did the first one.

"I want the full hour session today," Clancy said.

The commander of the Fifth Precinct handed the young man the empty glass. Then, he rose from the couch, entered the bedroom, and closed the door behind him.

After Clancy had carefully removed his uniform and hung it in the closet, someone knocked at the bedroom door.

"Come in," Clancy said.

The young man with the straw-colored hair entered the bedroom holding two double scotches. He wore a blond shoulder-length wig.

And nothing else.

The End

www.ingramcontent.com/pod-product-compliance
Lightning Source LLC
Chambersburg PA
CBHW070544220526
45467CB00003B/1062